For Erik

I'm planning on spending eternity with you.

We'll ask God a lot of questions together.

The answers will be worth the tears.

TY GIBSON

Pacific Press® Publishing Association
Nampa, Idaho
Oshawa, Ontario, Canada
www.pacificpress.com

The author would enjoy hearing your response to this book.
To contact him write to:

Ty Gibson
PO Box 222
Malo, WA 99150

or

tygibson@lbm.org

GRAPHIC DESIGN BY MCM Design Studio, LLC.
COVER ILLUSRTATION BY Lars Justinen

Additional copies of this book may be purchased at
http://www.adventistbookcenter.com

All Scripture quotations are from the King James
Version unless otherwise noted. NKJV indicates the New
King James Version. NIV indicates the New International Version.
NASB indicates the New American Standard Bible. AB indicates The Amplified Bible.
NEB indicates the New English Bible. NCV indicates the New Century Version. RSV
indicates the Revised Standard Version.

All emphases and words in brackets within quotations are added by the author,
except in quotations from The Amplified Bible.

Names and details in stories have been changed to honor
the privacy of the individuals involved.

ISBN 13: 978-0-8163-1852-0
ISBN 10: 0-8163-1852-2

CONTENTS

Pervasive Grace: Embracing All

1
NAMELESS TEARS

ALL I HAVE TO do is close my eyes and I'm there . . .

I can see the large, three-story apartment complex, and the turquoise door with number 319 on it.

Home.

And I can see myself sitting in my room on the edge of my bed, knowing that a certain weird thing is about to happen . . . again. The door is shut and locked in order to spare myself the embarrassment of anyone walking in on me.

Most days were fine. I was a social kid, eager to spend time with my friends after school, skateboarding, hitch-hiking to the beach or just roaming the neighborhood.

When I say most days were fine, I mean as fine as things could be, given the circumstances. I was the oldest of four kids being raised by a single mom who worked 10- and 12-hour days as a waitress to keep us fed and clothed. Just behind us loomed the big, dark shadow of an abusive marriage and an ugly divorce. Los Angeles, California, was our world. The streets were my playground. While Mom was at work, life unfolded before me.

My days included routine encounters with drug dealers and addicts, shootings and stabbings, racial hatred and gang warfare, child abuse and all kinds of other messed-up stuff.

As for any positive spiritual influence, there was none in sight. The concept of God was foreign. We had no Bible in our home, or any other spiritual literature, for that matter. I knew about the rock band Genesis, but not the book of Genesis. I had never even heard of the Ten Commandments. Jesus was a remotely familiar name, but mostly in cursing.

Fine. Most days were fine. Such was life. There was nothing else. Nothing, that is, except those strange times alone in my room with the whole world shut out. There, by myself, I would periodically face a recurring phenomenon I desperately hated to experience. And yet, in a way, I clung to it, because it was the only thing that felt meaningful. It was like a distant pinhole in the blackness, allowing a thin shaft of light to enter, beckoning ever so provocatively. I groped toward it.

Toward what?

I didn't know.

I usually knew when it was going to happen. I could feel it building inside of me. During school I would sense myself pulling away from everyone into a quietness, an involuntary retreating not prompted by a conscious choice. When the final dismissal bell would ring, rather than rushing off with my friends, I would nervously make up some excuse and head home. Down the sidewalk as fast as my right leg could push my skateboard, off the board and running through the vacant field, over the fence, up the three flights of stairs, I would burst through door number 319 and into my room. Catching my breath, I'd sit on the edge of my bed awaiting the inevitable.

Then it would happen.

"What's wrong with me?" (Sigh).

I'd start to feel those familiar but undefinable feelings until tears would begin to well up in my eyes. Soon I would be weeping profusely, uncontrollably, for no apparent reason.

Nameless tears.

I call them *nameless tears* because that's what they were. Tears as passionate as a hurricane, but as unexplainable as quantum physics. If you had been there to ask me, "What's wrong? Why are you crying?" in all honesty I would have had to say, "I don't know." And yet, on some level beyond articulation, in a part of my heart as yet unfamiliar to me, I did know. At least I was beginning to know. With each repetition of the strange experience, I began to gain a more intelligible sense of my feelings. It was as if I were a fish on dry land gulping for water or a mammal underwater gasping for air. With increasing intensity I could sense the existence of a higher reality to which my heart belonged, but from which I was far removed. I hated my world and felt completely out of place in it. The violence, the racism, the sexual perversions and violations, the lying, the child abuse, the raw, unabashed selfishness—with every fiber of my being, I hated it all. And yet, I was part of it, for which I also hated myself.

But not only did I hate the world around me and the wrong within me, I also deeply longed for something different, something better, for myself and for the world. It was more than a nebulous desire. It was a distinct "knowingness," hazy at first but becoming more and more defined with each tear trickling down my cheeks and splashing to the floor. It wasn't merely a wish, like a five-year-old wishes for a Snickers bar the size of a house. I knew that there was, in fact, something true and good and beautiful beyond my scope of vision, if I could just find it. Or better yet, if it could just find me. With all the strength of my youthful passion, I yearned to be embraced by whatever was drawing me from afar.

Finally, the day of peace and resolve arrived. My tears began to catch the image of an approaching personage. The "what" for which I so deeply yearned turned out to be a "Who." God introduced Himself to me. Not face to face, but heart to heart. I didn't hear an audible voice, but the meeting was no less real for its silence. (For a more detailed account of my encounter with God, read chapter 1 of my book, *See With New Eyes.*)

In the very first hour of my encounter with God, I knew He was the definition of my heart's deepest desire. Everything began to make sense. All along, day and night without pause, I had been the fiercely-loved object of a Supernatural Being. Although I was without any religious instruction to guide me, and had not even the slightest knowledge of God's existence or character, He aroused in me a distinct awareness of the difference between right and wrong, a longing for something better, and a conviction that there was, indeed, something better out there somewhere. While I had been wholly unconscious of Him, He was actively pursuing my heart with ingenious orchestration and relentless passion. The meaning of my tears became clear.

Later on I would read and understand what had happened to me, clearly explained by the apostle Paul:

" 'He has made from one blood every nation of men to dwell on all the face of the earth, and has determined their preappointed times and the boundaries of their dwellings, so that they should seek the Lord, in the hope that they might grope for Him (feel after him, KJV) and find Him, though He is not far from each one of us' " (Acts 17:26, 27, NKJV).

What an astounding and comforting reality!

Do not miss what Paul is saying here. The Almighty God, who is above and beyond us all, broods over us with "hope." He is hoping, this lofty yet lowly One—desperately, deeply hoping—that each person will "feel after Him and find Him." And He doesn't just sit back on His throne inactively hoping. Rather, He is intimately, personally, aggressively involved in every life. By His wise and calculated providence, He has "determined" the ebb and flow of each individual history, the very place we live and the influences we encounter. All we experience transpires under His loving guidance.

"So that . . . "

Paul makes it clear that God orchestrates the circumstances of every life with a specific purpose in mind: "*So that* we might feel after Him and find Him." Not that He is hard to find, Paul hastens to add, for "He is not far from each one of us." And if not far, then He is near. Near to whom? To "each one of us"; that is, to every single man, woman, and child who has ever existed on planet Earth, during every year and month and day and hour of human history, in every nation and city and home and room. No one has ever escaped His compassionate notice. No one has ever slipped through His fingers. All receive the utmost personal attention. With deliberate intent God has always been near every individual, hoping to be felt for and found.

How near?

Paul answers: "For in him we live, and move, and have our

being" (Acts 17:28). Consistent with Paul's previous statement that God is "not far from each one of us," the "we" here is clearly inclusive of the entire human race, for it involves all who "live" and "move" and "have being." So though it may seem awkward to say so of even unbelievers, there is a sense in which every human being is "in Him." This is the intimate language Paul employs to define God's nearness to "each one of us." Certainly it does not mean that every person is eternally saved, nor is it a reference to any kind of mystical idea that every person is a small particle of God. Rather, the statement that we are "in Him" refers to the sublime truth of our existence by His choice and power. "In Him"—within the desire of His will and the purpose of His goodness—we have life; we experience the movements of life in mind, emotion, will, and body; and we have the "being" of individual personhood and character. We live and move and have identity because God wills it. "He is before all things, and *by him* all things consist" (Colossians 1:17). "*In him* all things hold together" (NIV). Whether we know Him or not, acknowledge Him or not, thank Him or not, the life we live, along with all our abilities, privileges, and blessings, is the gift of God's grace moment by moment.

"Here is what I have seen," declares wise King Solomon, "It is good and fitting for one to eat and drink, and to enjoy the good of all his labor in which he toils under the sun all the days of his life which God gives him; for it is his heritage. As for every man to whom God has given riches and wealth, and given him power to eat of it, to receive his heritage and rejoice in his labor—this is the gift of God" (Ecclesiastes 5:18, 19, NKJV).

Life itself continually emanates directly from God as a free gift to all. The very capacity to work and produce and enjoy the good things of life, even the simple ability to eat and relish food, is an ongoing manifestation of the ever-outreaching grace of God's benevolent character. Every time we encounter something true, experience something good, or behold something beautiful, God is revealing Himself with the passionate hope that we will "feel after Him" as the source behind all blessings.

But why does He want us to feel after Him and find Him?

Because as our Father-Creator, He has designed the inner workings of our minds and emotions to survive and grow and soar with eternal pleasure by means of receiving and giving His love. This most basic and profound reality of our existence is articulated beautifully by the apostle John:

"God is love. Whoever lives in love lives in God, and God in him" (1 John 4:16, NIV).

Selfless, other-centered love is the fundamental essence of God's character. Out of that essence He created mankind "in his own image" (Genesis 1:27). We were made for love. The fall of humanity into sin basically consisted of a choice to cease living in the image of God's love and to venture into the dark realm of living for self, which turns out to be an attempt at the impossible, due to the very nature of life as God has engineered it. One cannot live for self and really live life as it is meant to be. Living for self imposes guilt, erodes self-respect and eventually destroys the very will to continue living. Selfishness, by its very nature, is detachment and isolation from all others, most tragically from God, the Source of life and love.

Redemption is all about healing the problem of selfishness in the character of man through a restoration of divine love in the soul;

for love, by nature, is connection and integration with others, most vitally with God. Therefore, John reasons, to live in love is to live in God. The divinely intended meaning of our existence is—simply, profoundly—a love relationship with God and His creation. Restoration to vital union with our Maker involves the restoration of His love in our otherwise "self-*sin*-tered" lives, liberating us from the deep-seated derangements of sin in our characters.

God longs for us to feel after Him and find Him because He loves us with all the energy of His divine being. It is the nature of His love to continually reach out of Himself in tireless efforts to secure our eternal happiness, which is only possible as we embrace His love and allow it to flow freely out of our lives to Him and all others.

I still cry. In fact, I just shed tears yesterday. But now my tears are named.

They are tears of longing for more of God: "As the deer pants for the water brooks, so pants my soul for You, O God. My soul thirsts for God, for the living God" (Psalm 42:1, 2, NKJV).

They are tears of joy for the pleasure of knowing His love: "In Your presence is fullness of joy; at Your right hand are pleasures forevermore" (Psalm 16:11, NKJV).

They are sometimes tears of sorrow for the times I ignore Him or misrepresent His beautiful character: "Be merciful to me, O Lord, for I cry to You" (Psalm 86:3, NKJV).

I still cry.

Do you?

Pause right now to identify your own tears. If they are yet nameless, recognize that your deepest heart-longings are for an intimate, eternal relationship with the divine Lover of your soul. If they are named, then I welcome you home to the heart of God.

Father-Creator: Thank You for finding me in apartment 319, in my room. I was completely oblivious to what was going on in my heart. It is truly an incredible and wonderful thing to finally realize that it was You all along, every step of the way, with every tear I cried. It was You drawing my soul with the powerful current of Your love. You were introducing thoughts into my mind and feelings into my heart. You were whispering inaudible words of truth and goodness and beauty into my darkened soul. What a powerful dawning it was when, finally, the truth burst upon my consciousness, that I was the deeply-loved object of the Almighty God's tireless labors to bring me to Himself! Thank You for arousing in me the unquenchable desire to "feel after You." Joyfully in Christ, Amen.

2
NAMELESS SAVIOR

STANDING THERE in the art gallery, I was transfixed in deep thought. The striking painting was preaching to me—a sermon I had never heard. I tried to listen very carefully. If ever a picture was worth a thousand words, the one hanging before me certainly was. Far more than a thousand words, in a few moments of time this "masterpiece" communicated to my heart an eternity of beauty concerning the character of God.

Look at it with me.

In the receding landscape there is a smoldering farmhouse and barn. The flames of Indian warpath have burned down the white man's home.

Prominent in the foreground are two blond-haired, blue-eyed children. Lone survivors. The boy is about six or seven. The girl is maybe a year or two younger. Big brother is holding little sister's trembling hand as they both stare, frozen with terror, at two galloping horses rushing toward them carrying Indians painted for war.

One of the horses is slightly in the lead. The warrior on its back wears a look of savage hatred on his face. His arm is lifted high with a tomahawk ready to swing downward at the terrified little girl. In a split second her head will be severed from her shoulders.

But there is another influence at work, a power contrary to hatred and in favor of love.

The second horse approaches with what appears to be greater speed, bearing an Indian brave whose countenance is flooded with desperate compassion. He raises his hand in front of his fellow warrior's arm to prevent the murder of the innocent.

The message is clear.

Do you see it?

Do you hear it?

God is a very present and pervasive influence in every human experience. No one has ever or will ever be passed over by the passionate pursuit of His saving love. The gravitational pull of His grace has drawn upon every heart, throughout all of history, regardless of one's level of theological knowledge or religious circumstances.

And yet, the New Testament boldly asserts of Jesus Christ, "Neither is there salvation in any other: for there is none other name under heaven given among men, whereby we must be saved" (Acts 4:12). How are we to understand this apparently narrow passageway into eternal life—through faith in the name of Christ alone—given the fact that He is a relatively new figure in human history? Thousands of years transpired before He was born. Countless millions have lived and died before and after His time having never so much as heard His name. We are logically driven to one of two startling conclusions: either (1) all who have never known Him by name are automatically lost due to the inescapable disadvantage of being born in the wrong place and/or at the wrong time, or (2) all who have ever lived have received ample enlightenment for eternal salvation whether they have encountered the historical person of Jesus Christ or not, the Savior having introduced Himself to them in some other way on some different level.

One of the most amazing and comforting declarations of the Bible proclaims that Jesus Christ is "the true Light, which lighteth every man that cometh into the world" (John 1:9). At first glance this statement may seem to be a gross exaggeration. Its claim appears extreme. How can the Bible dare to say Jesus has enlightened *every* person who has come into the world, when, in fact, most of the human population throughout history never heard of Him?

The answer is evident in the immediate context. The apostle John ascribes to Christ an existence and an active involvement in our world that predates His life as a man on earth. In His preincarnate existence, He was "the Word" and "the Light" of God to all people. Notice John's explanation:

"In the beginning was the Word, and the Word was with God, and the Word was God. . . . In him was life; and the life was the light of men [mankind]. And the light shineth in darkness; and the darkness comprehended it not [did not prevail against it]. . . . That was [in all times past] the true Light, which lighteth every man that cometh into the world" (John 1:1, 4, 5, 9).

As the ever-present, always-speaking "Word" of truth, Christ has actively communicated to all human hearts in all times, to those who have known Him by name *and* to those who have not. When King Solomon personified "Wisdom" in the book of Proverbs, he was prophetically referring to "the Word," the "true Light," that was eventually to be incarnate in the divine-human person-age of Jesus Christ (Proverbs 4 and 8). Solomon described Wisdom as a self-evident principle always crying out in our human experience, constantly calling each of us into harmony with its righteous ways. Reading Proverbs 8 gives the distinct impression that the "Word" of "Wisdom" is inescapable, resounding, and universal. All hear Wisdom's voice speaking in their inner consciousness. All hearts resonate with her indisputable truth. And all must either embrace or resist Wisdom's declarations. Moving down through time from Solomon's day, we discover that the apostle Paul identified the incarnate Jesus Christ as "the wisdom of God" (1 Corinthians 1:24). It was He of whom Solomon wrote.

Moses put forth the same concept: " 'For this commandment [the Word of God] which I command you today, is not too mysterious for you, nor is it far off. It is not in heaven, that you should say, "Who will ascend into heaven for us and bring it to us, that we may hear it and do it?" Nor is it beyond the sea, that you should say, "Who will go over the sea for us and bring it to us, that we may hear it and do it?" But the word is very near you, in your mouth and in your heart, that you may do it' " (Deuteronomy 30:11-14, NKJV).

Incredibly, Moses tells the children of Israel that God's Word of truth is resounding in their very own hearts and mouths, if they will but acknowledge it and listen. "Stop and think clearly," he seems to be saying, "and you will find that the truth I am telling you is self-evident, having been built by God into your very nature. It is not foreign or strange to you, if you would just stop and recognize the voice of God's truth constantly speaking to your heart. Before you even heard me explain it to you, the Word was already very near to you; so near, in fact, that it is what you know to be truth in your inmost heart, because God has been speaking to you all along."

Just as he does with Solomon's personified Wisdom, the apostle Paul quotes this passage of Moses and applies it directly to Christ (Romans 10:5-10). Not only *is* Jesus the Word of God, but He always *has been*. Never has He been silent. All of the wisdom of eternal truth is embodied in Him, and that wisdom has ever been crying out in our dark world. The true Light has always shined, and the darkness has never prevailed against it. Before His glorious incarnation, when "the Word was made flesh, and dwelt among us" (John 1:14), He was the wordless Word, whispering with thunderous silence in all hearts throughout history. In a very real sense, the enlightenment of Christ penetrates every soul, without exception.

Certainly this biblical truth is not intended to imply that all people have encountered the Christian faith. Most have not. Countless men and women have lived and died in complete ignorance of Jesus by name, and yet, He is the Savior of the world (John 3:16; 1 Timothy 4:10), known in principle to all who have acknowledged His Word in their hearts and embraced whatever light they could see. In those matters of truth and righteousness of which they were ignorant, "God winked" with tender mercy (Acts 17:30). It is true that great spiritual darkness is evident on every page of the human story. Yet, God's love is too great to be limited by such circumstances. "Where sin abounded, grace did much more abound" (Romans 5:20). While it cannot be said that all people have known all truth, it must be true that sufficient spiritual blessings, adequate for eternal salvation, have been lavished freely upon all without exception. For many people, Christ has been a nameless Savior, One whom they have known by His character, His love, His principles of truth and wisdom. They will know Him by name on resurrection morning.

It is right here, on resurrection morning, that my imagination picks up where the painting in the gallery left off. I'll be waiting for you in the next chapter.

Gracious Father of us all: What peace and joy settles upon my soul as I realize that not one of my fellow human beings has ever been passed over by You! Truly Your Word is resounding in every heart. I heard it myself before I ever opened a Bible. Whether in character or by name, Christ has introduced Himself to every man, woman, and child. I'm so eager to meet the many who will live for eternity in Your kingdom. With the Word in my heart and on my lips, I pray. Amen.

3
A STRANGE QUESTION IN AN UNFAMILIAR PLACE

WHEN WE GET to heaven, there will be some people asking Jesus a strange question. It won't seem strange from their standpoint. To them, it will be a perfectly logical thing to ask. But to you and me, it will be a bit odd, because we will never ask such a question. Here it is, tucked away in an Old Testament prophecy:

"And one shall say unto him, What are these wounds in thine hands? Then he shall answer, Those with which I was wounded in the house of my friends" (Zechariah 13:6).

Can you picture the scene?

There we are in heaven. We're all rejoicing to be with the Savior at last. Then someone says, "Excuse me, but why are those scars on Your hands?"

You won't ask such a question. Neither will I. We know the reason for the scars. We've read the account of His crucifixion and heard the story over and over again. But evidently there will be people in heaven who don't know and haven't heard. Jesus won't be surprised by their question. He will be expecting it and will no doubt be eager to explain the meaning of His wounds.

During His earthly ministry, the Savior told us that many such people would be eternally saved. The account is recorded in Matthew 8:5-11. A gentile centurion came to Jesus to request healing for his servant. Jesus eagerly responded, "I will come and heal him."

"The centurion answered and said, Lord, I am not worthy that thou shouldest come under my roof: but speak the word only, and my servant shall be healed."

Jesus was so impressed that He said to the Jews standing around, "I have not found so great faith, no, not in Israel."

Try to imagine the setting. The Jews regarded themselves as spiritually superior to all other people. As far as they could see, which wasn't very far, they alone were favored of God; they alone would find a welcomed entrance into the kingdom of God. Gentiles were regarded with contempt and were expected to be lost, with the exception of those few, who, against the tide of Jewish pride, converted to Judaism. So what must the atmosphere have been like when Jesus declared that this Gentile centurion had greater faith than He had witnessed in any Jew? Tense, to say the least. But that was nothing compared to what Jesus said next:

"And I say unto you, that many shall come from the east and west, and shall sit down with Abraham, and Isaac, and Jacob, in the kingdom of heaven." Luke's gospel adds, "from the north, and from the south . . . And, behold, there are last which shall be first, and there are first which shall be last" (Luke 13:29, 30).

Everyone who stood there listening to these words of Jesus knew exactly what He meant. North, south, east, and west of

Israel took in all of Europe and the vast Roman Empire, Asia, India, and Africa, indeed the whole world. Christ was actually saying that people from every nation and race would be eternally saved, apart from any contact with or even knowledge of the Jewish religion.

When the apostle John was given a vision of the many who will enter the kingdom of God, he saw "a great multitude, which no man could number, of all nations, and kindreds, and people, and tongues," standing "before the throne, and before the Lamb" (Revelation 7:9).

There will be many in the kingdom who lived before the time of Christ. Not only Jews, who looked forward to the coming of the Messiah by the testimony of the prophets, but also many others from every nation and language group on earth. There will also be many there who have lived after the time of Christ but never encountered a missionary or heard the gospel preached by human lips.

African tribesmen and women.

Asian sages and their disciples.

Indian seekers.

Eskimos and Arabs.

Vikings and Celts and Brits.

Incas and Aztecs.

Aborigines and Apaches.

On resurrection morning the vast, numberless throng of redeemed humanity will be composed of people who will know the meaning of the scars on the Savior's hands, and of those who will need to ask.

Picture the scene with me.

The great warfare between good and evil is finally over. Every person's eternal destiny is fixed. The confusion and chaos of earth's final days is giving way to the glorious event of Christ's second coming. Humanity's dark saga is forever ended.

There He is, the King of kings and lord of lords, in full view of all who are alive at His appearing. Surrounded by a numberless host of angels, He approaches, drawing nearer and nearer, until the entire heavens are filled with the brightness of His presence as a canopy of light. Those who are "alive and remain" of His faithful followers tremble, not with fear, but with pulsating joy.

"There He is," they whisper one to another.

"It's actually happening. Jesus Christ is here. He has come, just as He promised."

"Look at His face, His eyes so glowing with eager love."

As we stand there, arms outstretched and eyes riveted with adoration upon His beautiful countenance, the earth begins to quake. Then, suddenly, it happens—the resurrection of the saved of all ages. Everywhere we turn, joyful reunions are occurring. Family members and friends are embracing one another. Every face is flooded with joy.

But then I notice, in the vast multitude, faces here and there that seem different. Joyous, yes, joyous like all the others, but also somewhat perplexed, as though they are trying to understand a great riddle. As I look toward Jesus above us, He seems to have a special interest in these happy, bewildered ones. His eyes are eager to lock with theirs as He smiles at each one with unreserved welcome. Before I have a chance to ask the Savior who they are, at the beckoning of His musical voice we all feel our bodies lifting from the ground. In a moment we are with Him in the sky, mingling among the angels, flying away from earth's dark night of pain.

The next thing we know, the New Jerusalem, of which we have often read in Scripture, is our dwelling place. The beauty is beyond words. "A great multitude, which no man could number, of all nations, and kindreds, and people, and tongues" has entered into the indescribable bliss of God's presence. But there are many who seem more surprised than all the others—those unique ones I had noticed before. Again, before I can ask who they are, I observe Jesus taking special interest in them. The Light of the world is walking side-by-side with one after another.

Private conversations of some kind?

Not really private, but deeply personal.

Turning to a nearby angel, I ask, "Who are these people? I noticed them at the resurrection."

"They are men and women and children," the angel explains, "who never knew the Savior by name during their lives on earth. They are people from remote deserts and high mountain villages, from deep tropical jungles and crowded city jungles, oppressed men and women, abused children, ghetto kids, and many others who have known little more than suffering and uncertainty on earth. But in their pain and through their perplexity they heard the Savior's voice in their hearts. Each one said *Yes* to mercy, *Yes* to love, *Yes* to righteousness, and in so doing they said *Yes* to Him, their nameless Savior. He is now introducing Himself to them for the first time, by name, that is, and telling the story of redemption, the benefits of which they have experienced, but the facts of which they have never heard."

Knowing what my answer will be, the angel inquires, "Would you like to listen in?"

"Would I ever! Thank you!"

"Let's walk near them," the angel gestures me forward.

And the conversation I then hear causes me to weep with astonishment at the enormity of God's love.

"Who are You and where am I?" the amazed American Indian gentleman asks the majestic Man walking beside him.

"I am Jesus Christ, Your Creator and Savior . . ."

"Who?"

"Jesus Christ, and this place is the New Jerusalem, your eternal home."

"And what are those scars on Your hands? Everything else is so perfect here. Please don't be offended at my questions," the Indian asks courteously. "I really am very glad to be here; it's wonderful. But I just want to understand. The last thing I remember is falling asleep during a serious illness that swept through the village of my people."

Jesus smiles.

"I will not be offended at your questions. I am eager to answer every one of them. Allow Me to explain."

Then the world's Redeemer proceeds to unfold the entire story as no one else can. Creation in the beginning. The rebellion of Lucifer. The fall of Adam and Eve. The crippling, descending cycle of moral degradation and its resulting suffering. The Flood. The rise and fall of empires. The chosen people. The patriarchs and prophets. The deepening darkness. And then, finally, the incarnation of God's love in His Son. His sinless life. His sacrificial death. His triumphant resurrection. His glorious second coming and the resurrection of all who ever responded in faith to His ever-speaking, still, small voice.

Jesus narrates the whole course of human history, escorting

His riveted listener to the climactic demonstration of God's love at Calvary, pointing to the scars on His hands as evidence of that love. Tears of humble gratitude well up in the Indian's eyes as the full reality of God's grace dawns upon his mind.

"But I was just an Apache warrior. I never heard this story . . . this truth. Why am I here with You? How did You save me?"

"While you were on earth," Jesus explains, "it was not your privilege to know Me by name, but you knew Me nevertheless. You were born to a time and place in which the full radiance of My light did not shine. And yet, you were not left in total darkness. My Spirit attended You all the days of your life, impressing your heart and teaching your mind, through Nature, through your experiences, even through your pain."

"Yes, yes," the Indian enthusiastically breaks in with understanding, "I remember many perplexities and many times of distinct realization."

"You will remember, also," Jesus continues, "being frustrated with all the injustice and evil that surrounded you."

"Yes, I do, so very well."

"Do you also recall an almost aching desire for something better, for things to be right and true and peaceful in your world? Do you remember feeling compassion for the downtrodden and reaching out to bring relief? Do you remember feeling regretful when you did wrong?"

"Yes, I remember all of those thoughts and feelings so vividly. I always wished things could be different. And I could hardly live with myself for the times I participated in the wrongs I despised in others. I felt so sorry for my offenses and the wrongs of others."

"It was Me, all along, moving in you, calling you to Myself. Those feelings of hatred and sorrow for your sins were My gift of repentance to you."

"It's all so amazing! I see now. It all makes sense. I knew in my heart that there must be a very good and loving God somewhere in the great sky above. You are the One."

"Yes," the Savior replies, "I am your Creator and Redeemer, and I do love you. Welcome into the eternal bliss of My kingdom."

The man bows down before Jesus and pours forth a torrent of passionate gratitude: "Thank You, thank You, for saving me by Your incredible grace! I love You with all my heart."

Then the Savior motions for someone in the distance to come near as He says one last thing:

"There is one more thing I want to say before you begin exploring your new home. Thank you for saving the lives of two of my precious little children. I want you to meet them, although they are not children anymore."

Just then, a man and a woman, with blond hair and blue eyes, approach with grateful smiles and extended arms.

Father of all the earth: I just love who You are so very much. What an incredible and all-embracing plan of salvation You have devised! It is going to be so great to spend eternity with countless men and women whom You have saved out of every time and culture of history. Because You have acted so fairly and lovingly to all, eternity will be completely restful under Your benevolent rulership. I will never have any reason to question Your changeless, immovable righteousness and love. I am so glad to be Your child, in Christ. Amen.

4
THE EXTRAVAGANCE OF GRACE

I'M ONE OF THOSE guys of whom people sometimes say, "The lights are on, but no one is home." I'm the proverbial "space cadet," the textbook case "daydreamer." I often miss my exit off the highway and only realize my predicament on an average of 22.5 miles later. I answer the phone on the fifth ring, just in time for the caller to hang up. I return a hello with delayed reaction. I lock my keys in the car. (I've mastered that coat hanger thing.) I drive three hours from home to catch an international flight without my passport, with a note written on my hand that says, "DON'T FORGET YOUR PASSPORT." I arrive at a weekend speaking engagement only to discover I have no socks or underwear in my suitcase. (Some inside info for my fellow airheads: Value Rite Drug Store, open 24-hours a day, has black or navy emergency dress socks for $2.50 a pair. Sorry, no undies.)

According to my loved ones, a look of vacancy sometimes

haunts my eyes. But I want to set the record straight: I am home. More importantly, the light is on in my head. It's always been on, even before I knew to call it light. Yes, I've also groped in darkness, but there has always been at least a slender shaft of light shining in through some opening in my soul.

The light is on in your head, as well, no matter what your family and friends may say. As we have already learned from John, chapter 1, the light of Christ is on in every human soul. It always has been. And the darkness of sin that clouds our vision of God's character has never succeeded in extinguishing the illuminating influence of Christ.

But there is more, far more, that Christ has done for humanity as a whole, apart from any movement or merit on our part. After explaining the pre-incarnate activity of Christ as "the Word" and "the Light" in all human hearts, the apostle John makes this enormous, encompassing, even extravagant claim on behalf of Christ:

"Of His fullness we have all received, and grace for grace" (John 1:16, NKJV).

The word "fullness" (*pleroma*, Greek) means completeness, totality, to finish or accomplish. The "all" in this text is clearly the entire human race, inclusive of every individual. The gospel proclaims a complete, unreserved, unconditional giving of Christ, and all that is in Him, to humanity as a whole. We could paraphrase the verse, "The totality of all Christ is, and all that is His to give, has been poured out upon all, grace upon grace, upon the entire human race."

The apostle Paul was deeply impressed with the same truth:

"He that spared not his own Son, but delivered him up for us all, how shall he not with him also freely give us all things?" (Romans 8:32).

Incredible!

Christ is the one gift in which all God's gifts are given. In giving His Son, the Father gave all He could possibly give. "All things" are "freely" given to "us" in Christ.

To whom?

To "us," Paul says.

Who is the "us"?

Those to whom Christ was given.

Well, to whom was He given?

To all the world—every man, woman, and child.

"For God so loved the world, that he gave his only begotten Son, that whosoever believeth in him should not perish, but have everlasting life" (John 3:16).

Yes, one must believe in Christ to whatever degree the Savior reveals Himself, either by name or in nameless character, in order to possess eternal life. But before there is any believing on the part of any single individual, there must be a complete giving on God's part to all. And so there is, in the divine-human person of Jesus Christ.

The "Word," which had been whispering the truth into all human hearts throughout history, "was made flesh, and dwelt among us" (John 1:14). Or as Hebrews 7:26 says, He "became us." To say He "became flesh" is to say He "became us," for we are, all of us, the flesh He became. He did not merely dwell "among" us, meaning in our geographical proximity. Rather, He literally dwelt within us, that is, in our very nature. By means of the Incarnation, God actually, literally, really became a human being. The divine Son of God was given to the human race as a full-fledged member. "Great is the mystery of godliness: God was manifest in the flesh" (1 Timothy 3:16).

The very fact that God "became us" in Christ logically makes the gift of salvation free *to all* before it can be made experientially personal *to any*. His humanity is the humanity of all, not merely of those who believe in and accept Him. "He came unto his own, and his own received him not" (John 1:11). Whether we receive Him or reject Him, He came to us, in us, as us, just the same. "But as many as received him, to them gave he power to become the sons of God, even to them that believe on his name" (John 1:12). To receive Him and believe on His name are vitally indispensable for entering into the personal experience of His salvation. And yet, if He had not first given Himself freely *to all,* there would be absolutely nothing to receive *for any.*

In previous chapters, we explored two of the unconditional dimensions of God's grace upon all human beings:

1. *Life.* Our very existence itself, which includes all temporal and spiritual blessings, is the gift of God through Christ to all. "In him we live, and move, and have our being" (Acts 17:28). "In Him all things consist" (Colossians 1:17, NKJV). The Father "hath blessed us with all spiritual blessings . . . in Christ" (Ephesians 1:3). Peter calls our very existence "the grace of life" (1 Peter 3:7). As such, we do not deserve it. Only by virtue of the merciful love of God do our hearts beat, our tongues taste, our minds think, our emotions feel, and our souls crave, from one moment of time to the next. You have been compassionately spared your rightful doom, as have I. Take a deep breath. Whether you believe in Him or not, whether you love Him or could care less, you are alive because Christ has intervened on your behalf, and mine, as

Savior. We exist because He wills our existence in the tender grip of His love.

2. *Light.* The Light of truth continually shining, the Word of wisdom endlessly speaking, is the free gift of God's grace in Christ to all human beings. "That was the true Light, which lighteth every man that cometh into the world" (John 1:9). Every knowledge of right, every repulse of evil, every hunger for goodness, every craving for beauty—all proceed from Christ to all people whether we acknowledge Him as the mainspring or not.

In this chapter we will explore a third dimension of grace— forgiveness.

Not only has God given the gifts of life and light to every person who comes into the world, but He has clearly flooded the world with His saving grace. No one is excluded. The apostle Paul says, "The grace of God that brings salvation has appeared to all men" (Titus 2:11, NKJV). Saving grace is a pervasive influence endlessly emanating from the divine heart to all who live and move and have being. The entire world is surrounded by a healing atmosphere of grace as truly as we are surrounded by the air we breath. As we are all partakers of the air, the sunshine and the rain, so we are all subjects of God's saving initiative in Christ.

But what does this mean in practical terms?

Simply this: If God were to hold us fully accountable for our sins, allowing the complete penalty of our rebellion to come upon us, mankind would be totally obliterated. The Bible poses this significant question: "If You, Lord, should mark iniquities, O Lord, who could stand?" Then the amazing answer is given: "But there is forgiveness with You, that You may be feared" (Psalm 130:3, 4, NKJV).

The clear implication is that no one could stand before the Holy One and live if He were not extending forgiveness on some kind of universal level. The fact that sinners exist at all is profoundly simple evidence that God's pardoning mercy is, in some sense, upon the world as a whole. Divine grace is a life-preserving reality operational toward every individual. "This I recall to my mind, therefore have I hope. It is of the Lord's mercies that we are not consumed, because his compassions fail not" (Lamentations 3:21, 22).

Now, before you freak out at this idea (you know who you are), please hear what the Bible is saying on this point, and what it is not saying.

No doubt about it, there is a clear biblical sense in which God's forgiveness is conditional upon our confession and repentance: "If we confess our sins, he is faithful and just to forgive us our sins, and to cleanse us from all unrighteousness" (1 John 1:9). However, this fact does not negate the equally vital truth that God's grace must have an objective dimension prior to any right-doing on our part. One Bible truth does not cancel out the other; when taken together, as a paradoxical (not contradictory) whole, they shed great light.

When you really stop and think about it, salvation only makes sense as a free gift when we see it given in Christ to all without condition, to be accepted into (not created by) the individual life by faith. Otherwise, salvation is not a free gift of grace at all, but rather the product of our repentance. If God forgives only in response to our repentance, then forgiveness is not of free grace, but rather of debt. In other words, God owes it to us. But the Bible doesn't teach this. It teaches, rather, that Jesus is "the

Saviour of all men, specially of those that believe" (1 Timothy 4:10). "He is the expiation for our sins, and not for ours only but also for the sins of the whole world" (1 John 2:2, RSV). Said a different way, in the person of Christ is accomplished *the fact* of salvation for the whole world. By believing that reality, the salvation that is accomplished in Him becomes *experientially activated* in us. We believe the fact; we don't make it. We embrace a salvation that is; we do not cause it to be. We receive by faith an achieved salvation; we do not create salvation by right-doing.

When we confess our sins and repent, we are doing so in the motivating light of God's pardoning, non-condemnatory love. His saving love, therefore, of necessity, must predate our repentance. As we become conscious of God's forgiveness, faith ushers us into a personal acceptance of His forgiveness through repentance. At that moment we enter into the life-changing experience of eternal life.

But (and this is a vital *but*) prior to our repentance, God in mercy does not count our sins against us, in the sense of not giving us what we are due. The full effects of sin have been stayed, preserving our *temporal life* so we might have ample opportunity to see and embrace His forgiveness unto *eternal life*. The grace of God leads Him to refrain from marking our sins against us, enabling us to "stand" before Him as recipients of temporal and spiritual blessings we do not deserve. The psalmist clearly calls this standing "forgiveness" (Psalm 103:3, 4). We are the beneficiaries of a gracious second chance. Thus Scripture testifies that Christ has "brought [both] life and immortality to light through the gospel" (2 Timothy 1:10). Both temporal, probationary life, as well as immortal life, are the purchased possessions of God's grace in Christ.

Paul explains it like this:

"Now all things are of God, who has reconciled us to Himself through Jesus Christ, and has given us the ministry of reconciliation, that is, that God was in Christ reconciling the world to Himself, not imputing their trespasses to them, and has committed to us the word of reconciliation. Now then, we are ambassadors for Christ, as though God were pleading through us: we implore you on Christ's behalf, be reconciled to God" (2 Corinthians 5:18-20, NKJV).

Follow Paul's reasoning. He begins by saying that "all things are of God." Everything that pertains to our salvation has its origin in Him. Therefore, He is the Initiator from start to finish in our redemption. Nothing originates with us or concludes with us. We do not start the process or end it. Everything we experience first had existence in Him, due to His grace. If all things that pertain to our salvation are of God, then it follows that all of those things must predate our experience in them. Our forgiveness must already reside in God's heart before it can penetrate our hearts.

With that foundation, Paul extends his inspired logic by informing us that God "has [past tense] reconciled us to Himself through Jesus Christ." Then the apostle identifies the "us" whom God has reconciled in Christ. "God was in Christ reconciling the world [not just believers, but the whole world] to Himself." Before reconciliation with God becomes an experiential reality in us by faith, it is an achieved reality in Christ for all the world, before anyone believes.

Then Paul tells us exactly how, by what practical means, God has reconciled the world to Himself in Christ: by "not imputing their trespasses to them." Or as the NIV puts it, "not counting men's sins against them." Before we do anything at all—repent, confess, or even believe—God has already done something extremely significant. He "has reconciled the world to Himself" by "not counting men's sins against them." Therefore, it can be said without exaggeration, "All things are of God." Every possibility of human boasting and merit is completely blotted out of the picture. Our salvation is God's accomplishment in the person of Christ.

And yet, Paul does not teach "Universalism," a theological word for the idea that all sinners will ultimately be eternally saved. What Christ has achieved *in fact* by living and dying in our humanity, must be actively accepted into the experience of each individual *by faith* in order for personal salvation to occur. When we see and believe that God has not counted our sins against us, having acted towards us in the spirit of forgiveness when all we deserved was condemnation and death, then we are personally reconciled to God unto eternal life. Therefore, the message to unbelieving sinners is, "be *ye* reconciled to God." He has already done absolutely everything He can. Now the call is for us to move into harmony with what He has done. The message is not, "Change your heart toward God so He will change His heart toward you," but rather, "God is already reconciled in His heart toward you; now, be ye reconciled to Him."

There is no need of change in God. He has already smiled upon us in Christ. The need for change is in us, and that change can only happen in the empowering light of His changeless love. God is not softened and molded by our goodness, but we by His. For "the goodness of God leadeth thee to repentance" (Romans 2:4). If our perception of His goodness is limited or darkened by any notion of self-dependence—I must do this, that, or the other thing in order to deserve, earn, or even prompt God's forgiveness—then genuine repentance becomes impossible. Then, what may look like repentance is really a self-centered attempt to extract salvation from a reluctant, condemnatory God who needs the stimuli of *our* right-doing to arouse *His*. On the other hand, when we see and believe God is so good that "while we were yet sinners, Christ died for us" (Romans 5:8), then we are moved, deeply and genuinely, to a repentance born of love. Self is forgotten and the desire to please and honor such a God as this becomes the one passion that triumphantly swallows up all others.

Now then, if God has done so very much, why do we need to do anything? And if we do need to do something, what is it? These questions are answered in the next chapter.

God of extravagant grace: What a wonder You are! You have done more than my heart could have ever dreamed. You have gone to such great lengths to save me. I shudder to think of what a dark place the universe would be if You were not the merciful, forgiving person You are. It is only by the sweet virtue of Your mercy that we are not consumed. I turn to You with all my heart and I rest. In Christ, I pray. Amen.

5
THE SLEEPING GIANT
WITHIN US ALL

My son Jason has a rare talent. He can completely seal off his nostrils with his upper lip. No hands.

I know what you're thinking: "No sweat. Anyone can do that."

Well, before your pride rises too high, too fast, I suggest you try it. Hopefully you're not reading this in a public place. But even if you are, it is a noiseless endeavor. Just make sure no one sees you. Maybe hold the book up in front of your face.

Ready? Go ahead. Try.

Hummmm.

Again. Try harder. Use all your facial muscles. Use your tongue if you need to, but no hands. Just lift your upper lip as high as you can and seal 'em off, airtight.

Uh-huh.

Just as I suspected. You can't do it.

Face it, you could devote your entire life to mastering this ability, but your efforts would never pay off. You could spend hours each day for years at the local gym doing upper lip exercises, but to no avail. So go ahead and give up and save yourself a lifetime of frustration.

Nostril-sealing-with-upper-lip is not the only unique ability in the world. Some few can breathe fine streams of air out of their eyes. Fewer still can turn their tongues over both directions, to the right and to the left. Some can wiggle their ears without touching them. While almost all can cross their eyes inward toward the nose, only a few can turn the eyes outward in the opposite direction toward the ears.

Why you and I were passed by in these matters, I don't know. Such is life. We can't all have everything going for us. So square your shoulders, sir; lift your chin, ma'am, and go forward, knowing that regardless of what you lack, there is at least one ability you do have that matters more than any other. Yes, you are favorably endowed where it really counts. No matter who you are, or whatever else you cannot do, inside your heart is the ability to appreciate and embrace God's saving grace. The Bible calls this ability *faith*. And you have it. All you'll ever need. Whether you are using it or not is another question (which we will address in a moment), but you do have it. Everyone does, without exception:

"God has dealt to each one a measure of faith" (Romans 12:3, NKJV).

Jesus is "the author and finisher of our faith" (Hebrews 12:2).

Many people born into this world lack wealth, or outward beauty, or physical strength, or shortness, or a high IQ, or a strong immune system. But no one, absolutely no one, is born into this world without faith. Each person, without exception or conditions, is endowed with the internal capacity to see and embrace God's healing love. Not only has God lavished upon us extravagant grace, free to all, but He has also placed within us the supernatural mechanism of faith by which we may lay hold of His saving grace.

God has given all He can possibly give, and done all He can possibly do to save us, short of violating our freedom. Our power of choice is the respected line over which He will not pass. So then, while faith is present in every heart, it is not automatically actuated without the conscious consent of the individual will. God wields no such remote control. He has given the gift, but He will not exercise it contrary to our personal power to decide on our own behalf, which leads us to a vital question: How, then, is faith awakened to the noble purpose for which the Creator placed it within our hearts? The Bible gives only one answer:

"Faith . . . worketh by love" (Galatians 5:6).

The word "worketh" in this text is from the Greek word *energeo,* which means to energize. Literally, Paul says, "Faith is energized by love." Residing in every human soul, faith is present as a sleeping giant of inestimable potential awaiting the electrifying stroke of divine love. It is easy to see, then, that since God's love is the energizing force that arouses faith to action, it follows that an understandable encounter with God's love is the paramount issue of importance in every human experience. To provide such encounters, to reveal the beauty of His character, has been the Creator's great quest throughout history in His relationship with mankind. There are four basic channels through which God's character is made known:

1. The continual speaking of the Word of eternal truth in our conscience (Romans 2:14, 15).

2. The testimony of order, beneficence, and beauty in nature (Romans 1:19, 20; Psalm 19:1-4).

3. The inspiration of the Holy Spirit speaking through wise men, sages, teachers and prophets, and especially through the Holy Scriptures (2 Peters 1:21; Matthew 2:1, 2; Isaiah 41:1-7; 49:10-13).

4. And finally, the zenith of divine revelation in the incarnation, life, teachings, death, and resurrection of Jesus Christ (Hebrews 1:1-3; 2 Corinthians 4:6; John 14:9).

The vital point is this: We are saved by God's grace alone; and the faith by which we lay hold of that grace is itself a gift. Far from anything we can take credit for, faith is the divinely-implanted capacity in the soul to believe in, and act upon, the revelations of God's saving love. "For by grace are ye saved through faith; and that [faith itself is] not of yourselves: it is the gift of God: Not of works, lest any man should boast" (Ephesians 2:8, 9).

This fundamental relationship between grace and faith drives us to a logical and rather delightful conclusion: faith is responsive to saving grace, not grace to faith. This means that the gift of salvation by grace must preexist our exercise of faith. Otherwise, we make faith out to be some sort of positive-thinking mysticism by which a person calls into existence a previously nonexistent reality. Faith merely sees, believes in, and gratefully embraces a salvation which is wholly of God. Faith, by definition, means to focus with trust on something outside of self. It must have an existing object or receiver in which to invest its confidence. Faith does not manufacture facts, but simply lays hold of already existing facts.

Therefore, the saving grace of God must be an existing, achieved reality in Christ before we can exercise faith to embrace it. We do not create or arouse grace in God by exercising faith. Rather, God awakens faith *in us* by revealing His grace, which predates our exercise of faith. From the standpoint of God's giving, "of His grace have we all received, grace upon grace," in the divine-human person of Jesus Christ. Absolutely everything needful for eternal salvation is present in Him. The fuel that ignites faith into action is the truth of God's "unearnable" love manifested in Christ. Notice Paul's articulation of this point:

"In Him [Christ] you also trusted [exercised faith], after you heard the word of truth, the gospel [good news] of your salvation" (Ephesians 1:13, NKJV).

We trust in Christ after we hear a certain word of truth. What is that word? It is the good news of our salvation. But how can we hear about our salvation before we have believed? In only one way: there must be something to believe before we can believe it. Our salvation must be a real and existing truth that can be told to us prior to our exercise of faith; for it is the telling of that very truth that enables faith to be exercised. God does not ask us to exercise faith first, promising He will then save us. Rather, He asks us to exercise faith in the salvation He has already wrought out for us in His Son without any participation on our part.

In Paul's understanding, our entire salvation, and everything that pertains to it, is God's grace-wrought achievement in the person of Christ. Within the framework of Ephesians 1, the apostle repeatedly emphasizes what God has done "in Christ." Notice:

The Father "has [past tense] blessed us with every spiritual blessing in the heavenly places in Christ" (verse 3, NKJV).

"He [the Father] chose us [every person] in Him [Christ] before the foundation of the world" (verse 4).

"He has made [past tense] us accepted in the Beloved [Christ]" (verse 6).

"In Him we have redemption through His blood, the forgiveness of sins, according to the riches of His grace" (verse 7).

All of these things—"every spiritual blessing"—exist "in Christ" before they exist in us. They are merely activated in us by faith, not created. Therefore, the entirety of our salvation is, indeed, by grace alone, through faith alone, in all that God has done for us in Christ. Faith does not change the heart of God, but rather leads us to rest in His changeless heart. Anything short of an accomplished salvation in Christ for all mankind makes God the responder and us the initiators of our own salvation, with Him saving us in exchange for our good overtures. But if "all things are of God"; if our faith itself is the free gift of God to every person; and if even the exercise of that faith is made possible by a divine energizing of His love, then we are truly the humble recipients of a free salvation. God is infinitely good to all, no exceptions, and none will be lost due to any lack of provision on His part. Only by persistent refusal and determined unbelief will anyone perish in sin's destructive grasp.

I think there are going to be a lot more people in the kingdom than we have imagined. We may be surprised at some of those we meet there. Then again, who knows, some folks may be surprised to see us there.

God of infinite grace: I thank and praise You for the gift of faith You have deposited in my heart. And I thank You for the revelations of Your love that energize it to action. Adoration wells up within me as I think about the great lengths to which You have gone to save me. I love You so very much, Lord. In Christ, I pray. Amen.

The Embodiment of Grace: Disclosing Reality

6
CIRCLE OF LIFE, LINE OF DEATH

PUSH THE REWIND button in your mind.

Go back as far as you possibly can. Draw upon all the information in your memory from what you have heard and read. Go back before your birth. Before the birth of your great, great, great grandparents. Before Rome and Greece and Persia and Babylon. Go back before Moses. Before Noah and the Flood. Before Adam and Eve.

You are now out of this world, and the information base for your imagination to draw upon is dwindling.

But you still know of an order of beings called "angels," who were created before mankind. So think of the angels, and then think of them no more. Go back even before their existence, and before the existence of all other created beings.

You have now crossed the boundary of time, as we know it, into eternity past.

What do you find?

There, in the furthest reaches of your finite imagination, you will find yourself pondering a single profound reality . . .

God . . . and God alone.

For if God is the Creator of all things, then He is, Himself, the only uncreated One, and must have existed alone before all creation. And yet, as you contemplate God as He once existed in uncreated aloneness, you will find yourself pondering another divine reality . . .

God "unalone," in divine togetherness.

While God was alone as God distinct from all things yet to be created, He was not alone in the sense of an isolated self. God is a plurality, as well as a singularity. The account of our world's creation reveals to our finite minds the musings of this One and only God: "Let us [plural] make man in our [plural] image" (Genesis 1:26). Not "I shall," but rather "Let Us." God is an "Us," not only an "I." Father, Son, and Holy Spirit. And so, a third reality is immediately evident . . .

God is love.

This is why it makes perfect sense for God to be a Triune "Us" and not an isolated "I." For love cannot exist in utter aloneness, but must, by nature, reach out of self to lavish its passion on others. Love necessitates the existence of more than one.

Now then, this God of love, who is an other-centered "Us," began to create in His image, which, like the plurality of His nature, makes perfect sense in light of the fact that the essence of His character is love. He creates because He loves, and in order to love. And so it should come as no surprise that this God of love, who was alone and yet never alone, said, "It is not good that the man should be alone" (Genesis 2:18). Therefore, God created man as an *us*, like Himself. "So God created man in his own image . . . male and female created he *them*" (Genesis 1:27).

But right here a potential problem presents itself. The nature of plural existence—of humanity being an *us* rather than an *I*—is that each person exists as an individual self and yet in inseparable connection with other equally individual selves. To be simultaneously conscious of myself and of others outside of myself gives me the options of self-centeredness or other-centeredness. Here is the wonderful reality of free will. By this ingenious arrangement, I am invested with the power of choice, through which love is possible; through which, also, there is the danger of selfishness. I am free to put self first or to put others first.

We now have before us the foundational elements of reality:

God . . .
>   alone and yet not alone.

Love . . .
>   selfless, other-centered love as the essence
>   of God's character.

Creation . . .
>   human beings made in the image of divine love,
>   each one an individual self coexisting with others.

Choice . . .
>   the power to live in harmony with God's love
>   or to live for self.

With this backdrop for an introduction, we are prepared to explore the nature of things as God has made them in the image of His love, the disharmonizing problem of sin, and His plan for complete atonement.

We tend to define *sin* in the limited sense of behavioral violation of rules stated and enforced by God, and *guilt* as His verdict of condemnation upon those who commit the violations. Certainly sin does include outward misconduct, and certainly God does condemn sin. But there is more to it than that. We must be careful not to allow our limited view of sin and guilt to become erroneous by failing to see the bigger picture, leaving us with a warped view of God's character.

The Bible says, "sin is the transgression of the law" (1 John 3:4). But what is the law? And why is it a problem to violate it? The Bible also says that sin is to "come short of the glory of God" (Romans 3:23). The "glory of God" is a Scriptural reference to the character of God, composed of many good attributes and encompassed in the single, chief attribute of love (Exodus 33:18, 19; 1 John 4:16). Therefore, when the Bible says sin is transgression of God's law, we must understand the law to be, as it were, a transcript of His character of love. The law is not an arbitrary set of rules made up at random by God to prove His authority over us, but rather a practical explanation of what love looks like in real life. This is why Jesus could summarize the Ten Commandments in terms of love for God and love for all our fellow human beings (Matthew 22:37-40). Sin, therefore, is anything contrary to the character of God; more specifically, anything contrary to His love. But let's not pass too quickly over this concept of love. When we speak of God's character of love, what exactly do we mean?

Unlike our rather muddled usage of the word *love* in today's vocabulary—I love my wife, I love avocados, I love my pet gerbil—the Bible uses the word to designate a very specific way of thinking, feeling, and behaving. Love means to live from a motive to put all others before self. It is the essence of God's nature to live a completely selfless, other-centered existence, and He created humanity to also live in this way—by the law of love.

"God is love," selflessly just and merciful in all His ways. He created the universe out of that identity, so that all of creation is designed to operate soundly, orderly, and eternally only in perfect harmony with the righteous principles of love that compose His character. Hence, love is God's law, the principle by which He lives. It is a law because it is not arbitrary, but based on reality as it is, governing life by its righteous principles. Love is the law by which God made and sustains life.

Then, in contrast, there is this thing called *sin*. Like love, the Bible also calls sin a "law" (Romans 8:2; 7:21-23). Sin is the opposite, antagonistic principle at war with the law of love. Do not view sin as merely an alternative way of living, which happens to be harmlessly different from God's way. God's way is the only way to live, not because He happens to be more powerful and can arbitrarily punish us if we don't comply, but because life is actually, intrinsically present only in God's way, which is the way of love. The problem with sin is that it is wrong, actually, essentially, inherently wrong. And it is wrong for good reason, not just because the One in charge doesn't like it. To be sure, God does not like sin, but He doesn't like it because of what it does to its victims, not because He is a picky control freak who decided to come up with a list of arbitrary rules to keep us under His thumb. Sin, by its very nature, is anti-life. It is intrinsically destructive. Hence the Bible calls it "the law of sin and death" (Romans 8:2). It is a law because it is a cause whose effect is death.

Once the nature of sin is understood, it is easy to see why sin is a law of death: sin is selfishness, the antithesis of love. As such, it leads inevitably to the exclusion of, and isolation from, the sustaining love and support of all others, for sin always involves acting against others for the preservation and/or exaltation of self. Every particular sin warned against in God's law of love is selfishness at root level. A person commits murder to gain something for self, or to eliminate a threat to self, with an obvious negative outcome to the victim. A person commits adultery for the fulfillment of selfish sexual or emotional desire, with no real regard for those who will be injured as a result. A person lies to save face or secure an impression favorable to self, at whatever expense to those who will believe them. You name the sin, any sin, and with a little thought it will become clear that selfishness is at its foundation.

Allow me to develop the concept of law and sin with a simple illustration. God created the universe to function as a circle, Himself at the center of the circle as the original Source of life and love and every good thing. We receive all things from Him and, in turn, were made to revolve around Him in an ebb and flow of selfless giving to others:

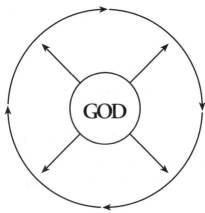

Sin, on the other hand, may be depicted as a departure from God's circle of beneficent love. Once separated, sin operates in the sinner as a lonely line rather than a circle:

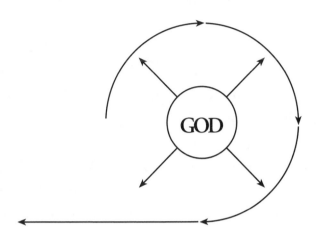

Moving out from the circle of giving and receiving, the natural impulse is to take and retain rather than give and receive. At first, selfishness imparts an illusionary sense of fulfillment, deceiving the mind with the idea that looking out for Number One is the only way to survive. But the feeling is, indeed, illusionary and fades with time as reality sets in, which leads us to the matter of guilt.

Because God's love is the law of the universe, by which He created and sustains all things, the principles of that law are designed into our very natures. Within our psycho-emotional makeup, love is encoded as the law of life. When we violate that law, a malfunction signal issues a warning in the form of guilt. That part of our minds we call *conscience* senses discomfort with sin and identifies it as a destructive virus in the computer system, so to speak. Guilt is not arbitrarily imposed by God any more than His law of love is arbitrary. He is the Architect of conscience, but He is not the source of guilt. He made us with the capacity to feel guilt as a merciful and wise deterrent to sin, desiring, of course, that we would never experience its pain.

A comparison may be made to the sensation of physical pain. If you put your hand on a red-hot wood stove, you will feel the pain of the destruction that is beginning to occur. Without pain, the destruction of your hand is sure. But the pain serves as a helpful warning that something is wrong, creating the natural impulse to pull your hand away from the source of heat. Your hand is injured, but saved. Even though it hurts, you are thankful for the ability to feel pain. You conclude, upon reflection, that pain is a very wise divine invention. The same is true of disease. Illness is attended by pain. We hate the pain, but we need it to tell us something is wrong so we can get help. If there were no pain involved in disease, we would simply drop dead one day without notice, with no opportunity to solve the problem. God is not the source of the pain, although He did create the physical laws that make pain possible.

While God does not desire that anyone ever experience physical pain or the psychological pain of guilt, even more so He does not desire our utter destruction. Pain is a built-in mercy mechanism intended to aid in the preservation of life. Pain is not an indication that God is exercising some kind of power above, beyond, or contrary to His law of love in order to inflict suffering as an arbitrary punishment for sin. Punishment is organic to sin itself. The only thing pain reveals of God's character is that He really loves us and wants us to live, so much so that He designed us in such a way that the warnings against sin are loud and clear. God has made it literally difficult for us to destroy ourselves. As in the physical realm, so in the spiritual: guilt is a merciful, divinely designed warning that what we are touching is hot and destructive, that sin is wrong and will affect our total ruin if we don't find a way to escape its influence.

It is commonly thought that the connection between sin and death is simply that if we don't repent of our sins God will kill us. Often no actual, intrinsic relationship is discerned between sin and death. But even a casual consideration of Scripture on this point persuades us otherwise. Notice just these few examples:

"A man reaps what he sows. The one who sows to please his sinful nature, *from* that nature will reap destruction; the one who sows to please the Spirit, *from* the Spirit will reap eternal life" (Galatians 6:7, 8, NIV).

"Sin . . . *leads* to death, . . . What benefit did you reap at that time from the things you are now ashamed of? Those things *result* in death! But now that you have been set free from sin and have become slaves to God, the benefit you reap *leads* to holiness, and the *result* is eternal life. For the *wages* of sin is death, but the *gift* of God is eternal life in Christ Jesus our Lord" (Romans 6:16, 21-23, NIV).

"For to be carnally minded *is* death" (Romans 8:6).

"For if you live according to the sinful nature, you will die" (Romans 8:13, NIV).

"He who misses Me or sins against Me wrongs and injures himself; all who hate Me love and court death" (Proverbs 8:36, AB).

"Sin, when it is full-grown, gives birth to death" (James 1:15, NIV).

All of these Scriptures portray an organic relationship between sin and death. Sin is set forth as a law, or power, which itself gives birth to death. It is a sowing and reaping principle. Plant carrot seed in the ground and carrots will grow for eventual harvest. Nobody plants carrot seed and then expects God to drop a bag of carrots from the sky as a reward for planting the seed. To the contrary, we understand that there is an actual connection between the act of planting and the eventual reaping. Can it be said that the carrots that grow from our planting are a blessing from God? Absolutely! Why? Because God created and sustains the laws that cause the whole process to work.

So, when Paul says that holiness results in eternal life, he is not removing God from the equation and making life a mere naturalistic cause and effect matter. He is simply describing *how* God gives us eternal life. God is the One who, in His infinite wisdom, established the laws that govern life. And He has ordained that eternal life can only happen through holiness, that is, through love-motivated harmony with the principles of His law.

The same is true on the negative side of reality. Just as the principles of love lead to life, so "sin, when it is finished, bringeth forth death" (James 1:15). "As righteousness tendeth to life, so he that pursueth evil pursueth it to his own death" (Proverbs 11:19). When the Bible says, "the way of transgressors is hard" (Proverbs 13:15), it does not mean, for example, that if you drink alcohol and drive, God will send an angel to push your car into oncoming traffic. It means, rather, that the alcohol will impair your judgment and balance, which could cause you to lose control of your car and wreck. It doesn't mean that if you smoke cigarettes for twenty years, God will miraculously create cancer in your body;

but rather that smoking causes cancer. The same holds true for all sin and suffering, and for sin in its ultimate outcome of final destruction.

Are we to conclude, then, that God never interposes to take life by a direct act on His part? Certainly not. There are clear examples in Scripture of God exercising His power over creation to end life: the Flood; the destruction of Sodom and Gomorrah by fire; the swallowing up of Korah, Dathan, and Abiram by an opening in the earth; Ananias and Sapphira dropping dead in Peter's presence for lying.

All of these are situations in which God has taken life. It is important to note that in each instance there was a context which persuades us that God acted in loving justice. Even in our human judicial systems, we can accept the death penalty in extreme cases. If a man commits brutal crimes and is sentenced to death, we do not regard the judge, the jury, or even the one who pushes the button on the electric chair, to be murderers. And yet, they have taken life. We understand there is a difference between just execution and murder. God has only taken life under the most severe circumstances, and with the highest motive of love in every case, for the best good of the victims and the victimizers. But even in such cases, the sin of those executed was tending toward death as its ultimate end, and God merely intervened for some loving purpose. So upon careful consideration, it becomes clear that God is the Author and Sustainer of life, and that death is an unwanted intruder in His universe, which has its origin in sin, not in Him. The Lord simply deals with the situation as it is, only taking life when allowing it to continue is more detrimental than to end it. Aside from these rare interventions on His part, the Scriptures teach that suffering and death are the result of sin. God does not threaten, "If you keep sinning, I will kill you." Rather, He warns, "If you continue in sin, you will die," for "sin, when it is finished, bringeth forth death." And so He pleads, "I have no pleasure in the death of the wicked; but that the wicked turn from his way and live: turn ye, turn ye from your evil ways; for why will ye die . . . ?" (Ezekiel 33:11). We're caught off guard by a question like this from God. We are more inclined to ask Him, "Why do You kill?" But He points to our sin and asks us, "Why do you choose death?"

Ultimately, laying aside our diversionary complaints about God occasionally executing justice by taking life, we must see that sin is a destructive force from which God has graciously provided refuge in Christ. He created us within the circle of His love for our eternal life and happiness. We have separated ourselves from that circle to pursue the illusion of life and happiness through self-serving. Because His character is unchanged by our affair with sin and death, He has encompassed us with an even larger circle of love—love extending itself as grace—to meet us in our need.

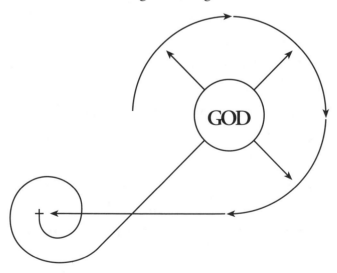

The ultimate end goal of the plan of salvation is to bring about complete atonement, a harmonizing oneness, between sinful human beings and a holy God; to restore us to life within the circle of God's selfless, other-centered love. Jesus Christ is the One sent by the Father to accomplish the atonement:

"We also joy in God through our Lord Jesus Christ, by whom we have now received the *atonement*" (Romans 5:11).

"For Christ also hath once suffered for sins, the just for the unjust, that he might *bring us to God*" (1 Peter 3:18).

"Who his own self bare our sins in his own body on the tree, that we, being dead to sins, should live unto righteousness: by whose stripes ye were healed. For ye were as sheep going *astray;* but are now *returned* unto the Shepherd and Bishop of your souls" (1 Peter 2:24, 25).

"For the love of Christ constraineth us . . . that they which live should not henceforth live unto themselves, but unto him which died for them, and rose again" (2 Corinthians 5:14, 15).

Please notice the reoccurring point in the preceding verses:

- Through Christ we receive "atonement"; we are made one with God.
- The purpose of the substitutionary death of Christ is to "bring us to God"; not Him to us. God has demonstrated His reconciled position toward us in Christ.
- Through sin we have gone "astray"; but through the sacrifice of Christ we "are now returned" to God.
- The love of Christ, revealed in His death, causes us to cease living for self and to start living for Him; we are reestablished in the circle of selfless, other-centered love through the atoning death of Christ.

In the chapters that follow we will explore in greater detail the practical hows and whys of the atonement. We have only introduced the topic here. Our first interest will be to contemplate the embodiment of God's atoning grace in Christ. Then, in the third and final section of the book, we will delve into the experiential impact of that grace in the believer's life.

Creator of the circle of endless love: I am in breathless awe at who You are and the way You have made things. When I look honestly inside myself, it is painfully clear that I have tried to live outside of the circle of Your love. I am self-centered to the core. But You have encompassed me within the larger circle of Your grace in Christ. I pray that You will stop at nothing to fully reconnect me to Your universe. Why do I even ask such a thing, as though You have not? Rather, open my sin-darkened eyes to see all that You have done. Riveted on Christ, I pray. Amen.

7
THE BEAUTY IN THE EYE OF EVERY BEHOLDER

"I HAVE ONLY FELT the way I feel tonight one other time in my life . . ."

Alexander was a fairly large man with a loud voice—drunk and out of control the first time I met him. He came into the theater where I was conducting a series of meetings in the city of Madonna, Latvia. There was a ruckus in the area where he was sitting. Or was he standing? Some of both. Voices rose in volume. Other attendees were trying to argue him out of the building due to his noisy, inebriated condition. They were actually making more noise than he was in their efforts to silence him. But he would not leave. I put forth my best effort to proceed with the presentation without visible distraction. As soon as the meeting was over, I moved as quickly as possible through the crowd to have a word with the noise-maker and his sober helpers. When our eyes met, I knew God had led him to the meeting.

"I am Alexander," he said with a deep slur.

"Pleased to meet you, Alexander. I'm Ty. I appreciate your coming tonight." (I don't think that was a lie. My appreciation was in the process of evolving.)

The exasperated people standing around began to whisper.

"Will you be able to attend tomorrow night?" I asked, placing my hand on his shoulder.

"They don't want me to come," he said, pointing to the many frowners in the crowd.

"But I want you to come. I'm inviting you as my guest. Please feel welcome to sit on the front row."

He looked perplexed and hesitated. Then, gazing around with a big smile, he said, " OK, I'll come." He was sobered by the idea that I actually wanted him to attend again. With that, we shook hands and he staggered away.

I wondered if Alexander would even remember my invitation. He did, and, as I hoped, he came sober. That night the topic of the presentation had a profound effect on Alexander. After the meeting, we visited. I can still see him sitting there in the theater seat with a wondering look on his face, trying to find a way to express his thoughts.

"I have only felt the way I feel tonight," he began, "one other time in my life—when my mother held me in her arms when I was a little boy after I was bad and I knew she still loved me. I don't believe in God. I'm an atheist. But if what you said tonight is true, it is the most beautiful thing I have ever heard. I find myself hoping it is true, wishing that such a God as I have seen tonight does exist."

Alexander was experiencing the irresistible drawing of which

Jesus spoke when He said, "I, if I be lifted up from the earth, will draw all men unto me" (John 12:32).

The word "draw" means *attract,* implying desirableness due to beauty. Jesus is here communicating that His sacrificial death reveals a beauty that will react upon every beholder to pull the heart to Him. But does Jesus really mean to say *all* will be drawn? Isn't that kind of stretching it? Shouldn't He have been more modest in His claim, hoping to draw at least some, perhaps even many? Certainly *all* who see the Cross are not drawn to Christ.

But notice, Jesus did not say all would believe or follow Him. He simply, profoundly said that all who see the Cross will be drawn. Yielding to the drawing is another matter. I believe Jesus meant that the revelation given at Calvary, whatever it is, strikes a responsive chord in every heart. No one can really look at what occurred at the Cross, understanding its divinely intended message, and not at least wish it were true, even if they choose not to believe it. For the cross of Christ has put on display a beauty that finds desire in the eye of every beholder.

Specifically, then, what is that beauty? What is so attractive about the Cross that it would exert such a magnetic influence upon every gazing soul? All that meets the biological eye is torn flesh and apparent defeat. Far from beautiful, the gory spectacle is enough to turn both the head and the stomach. So, where is the attraction?

Deeper!

In order to see the magnetic beauty of Calvary, we must look with the eye of faith beneath the bleeding body into the mind and emotions of the One hanging there. We must ask *the reason why* He submits to such agony and death. We must peer into the inner recesses of His heart to discern *the motive* that drove Him to endure such incredible suffering. Herein we shall discover *the deeper meaning* of the cross of Christ. And in its meaning we will behold its beauty and feel its drawing power.

> *The motive,*
>> *is the meaning,*
>>> *is the beauty,*
>>>> *is the drawing power.*

Probe with me.

The Cross echoes a resounding meaning and purpose, which hearkens back to our original design. By creation there is a divinely encoded message in every heart, a kind of DNA blueprint, speaking continually of a glorious past. This deeply etched encryption does not reside at the forefront of our consciousness. And yet we seem to know we are now far less than we once were, and we aspire to return to that mysterious past. Our hearts tell us we have fallen from some high position of moral standing, and we desire to be there again, to regain whatever we have lost. In our first parents, Adam and Eve, humanity was emotionally and psychologically engineered to live in a sort of symphonic harmony with the selfless, other-centered love that has its origin in the heart of God. "God is love" (1 John 4:8), and "God created man in his own image" (Genesis 1:27). The fall of Adam and Eve essentially meant a forfeiture of that love as the ruling principle of our existence. So the Cross makes deep moral sense to our runaway hearts. Like a person waking with amnesia after a serious head injury, we feel as though our true identity eludes us. As the amnesia victim

feels a strange sense of familiarity upon hearing her name or seeing a close friend, so we sense that we have come in contact with
the real meaning of our lives when we encounter the love displayed
at Calvary. A voice deep within us whispers, "I was made for this
kind of love, and it calls me."

The apostle Paul confirms that, indeed, the drawing power of
the Cross is in the love demonstrated there:

"For when we were still without strength, in due time Christ
died for the ungodly. For scarcely for a righteous man will one
die; yet perhaps for a good man someone would even dare to die.
But God demonstrates His own love toward us, in that while we
were still sinners, Christ died for us" (Romans 5:6-8, NKJV).

Paul makes three crucial points here:

1. The grammatical structure of the first sentence indicates
Paul's view that our lack of moral strength is a problem to which
the death of Christ is the divine solution. The Cross is God's empowering response to our condition of moral weakness. Having
made this point, Paul is about to explain how the Cross remedies
our impotence.

2. A contrast is then pointed out between two distinct kinds
of love: the highest form of fallen human love versus divine love.
The first is revealed when, on rare occasions, one human being
will willingly die for another human being he perceives as good,
someone thought to be worthy of such a sacrifice. "But God,"
Paul proclaims to emphasize the contrast, "demonstrates His own
love toward us in that while we were still sinners, Christ died for
us." In other words, God's love is of such a quality and depth that
it is unaltered by the fact that we are not good. We are sinners, in
fact, completely undeserving of even His tolerance, let alone His

love. He does not love us more when we do right, nor does He love us less when we do wrong. Such is the amazing nature of the love which continually pulsates in the heart of the infinite One.

3. So then, the demonstration of this love given in Christ at the Cross is the power by which God draws sinners. As Paul says in another place, "The preaching of the cross . . . is the power of God" (1 Corinthians 1:18). What kind of power? Motivational power! The power of His love moving within our hearts as we see the demonstration of His love for us in Christ.

"For the love of Christ compels us [propels us forward], because we judge [see or discern] thus: that if One [Christ] died for all, then all died [represented in Him]; and He died for all, that those who live should live no longer for themselves, but for Him who died for them and rose again" (2 Corinthian 5:14, 15, NKJV).

This is an incredibly clarifying passage of Scripture. Again, as in Romans 5:6-8, Paul says here that the love of God we see in Christ operates within us as a constraining, motivational force. So powerful is His love, in fact, that when we see and believe it, we begin moving in an entirely new direction—namely, to cease living for ourselves and to start living for Him in response to His self-sacrificing love. When we "judge," or discern, that Christ died for all, without exception, His love grips our hearts with transforming power. It is the for-all-without-exception nature of God's love which constitutes the power of the Cross, encompassing the entire human race, regardless of any measure of guilt and unresponsive to any degree of achieved righteousness. In Paul's Holy Spirit-inspired thinking, the death of Christ constituted the death of humanity as a whole in a representative sense, because He died as one of us, a member of the human family. Therefore, if all were taken up into the humanity of Christ, and thus all were represented in His death, we can only conclude—with unspeakable joy—that God's saving grace has enveloped all, with equal care and consideration, before we have done anything to deserve it.

Attractive, indeed!

Fallen human love is selective, according to Romans 5:7, only given to those we think are good or of practical value to ourselves. This means, of course, that we don't even really love those we have selected, but rather we love ourselves through them. Loving others because of derived value to self equates to selfishness, not love.

God's love is totally different. It is truly selfless and other-centered. Unlike fallen human love, God's love is not dependent on influences outside Himself, such as sacrifice or ceremony or good deeds of any kind. Nothing else besides His own identity was required to prompt Him to save lost humanity. His immediate, spontaneous response to our sin was, and is, to draw close and lavish grace upon us. Without hesitation or self-interest, as soon as Adam and Eve sinned, He reached out of Himself to seek and save us because it is His nature to do so. All the energies of His divine being were instantly channeled to our preservation and restoration. God's love was, and is, a sin-transcending, full-throttle reality, from the moment our first parents fell to this very moment and beyond.

This being the case, the suffering and death of Christ did not switch on God's love or activate His saving grace. Rather, the Cross is the visible demonstration, in time and space, of a love which has always been discernable to varying degrees through creation and in every conscience. At the Cross that love reached the zenith point of its revelation. But it was there all along in the heart of

God, streaming forth in an endless current of life and light to all. It is easy to see, then, how people in the generations prior to Calvary could be saved, for the sufferings of Christ did not incite God's saving grace, but merely disclosed—with climactic magnitude—the grace that was actively present toward all the world from the very inception of sin. The death of Christ did not make God favor us or induce Him to love us, but simply made it clear that He already did.

So then, when we encounter the cross of Christ, we are encountering God for who He is and always has been. We are face-to-face with divine love at the apex of its expression, the same love He originally put into us at creation. Having lost that love through sin, we yet long for it. The Cross holds it up before our searching eyes and draws us once more to where we belong.

And yet, there is a painful paradox. While our eyes are attracted to Him, they are also nervously averted. For we encounter more than God's beauty at the Cross. We also find ourselves face-to-face with our own ugliness. With this in mind, proceed to the next chapter with caution.

Precious Father: I am so powerfully attracted to You as I gaze upon Jesus. Truly You are beautiful beyond words. My heart yearns to be fully immersed in Your love. To see it more clearly. To embrace it more passionately. To reflect it more accurately. Flood me with Your grace. I ask in the light of Your love in Christ. Amen.

8
FROM WHOM WE AVERT OUR EYES

TRULY THE CROSS of Christ does reveal the beauty of God's character. But it also makes known the ugliness of our sin. He who would pluck the rose must also feel the thorns. The very One to whom we are so powerfully attracted is also the "One from whom we nervously avert our eyes" (Isaiah 53:3, personal paraphrase). A discomfort arises within us as we try to evade our shame and guilt. In order to gaze upon the Cross and believe its picture of God, we must of necessity be horrified and revolted by our sin, which brought Him there. His beauty is our humbling, if we will be humbled. But we find it difficult to believe He could be so good and we so bad. So unsettling, in fact, is the dual revelation of our sin in contrast to His righteousness, our selfishness raging against His love, that we often construct self-preserving theological paradigms to make Him look arbitrary and ourselves nearly victimized by a harsh justice, which is the figment of our imaginations. We attempt to protect ourselves from the truth of our sinful condition by believing that His sufferings and death were at the hand of God, rather than at our own hand.

Isaiah peered into this twisted, psychological dishonesty, when he wrote, "We saw His suffering and thought God was punishing Him. But He was wounded for the wrong we did; He was crushed for the evil we did." (Isaiah 53:4, 5, NCV). "We [ignorantly] considered Him stricken, smitten, and afflicted by God [as if with leprosy]. But He was wounded for our transgressions, He was bruised for our guilt and iniquities" (AB).

In this chapter, I'd like to ask you to take a deep breath, steady your heart, and open your mind as we explore the nature and magnitude of our sin alongside the nature and necessity of the atonement.

I have a poster that says something that shouldn't even need to be said.

"Two foundational facts of human enlightenment:

1. There is a God.

2. You are not Him."

Why would we need to remind ourselves of a truth so elementary and self-evident as this? Because somewhere in the root structure of our sin problem, there exists a deceived sense of self, which would really prefer that God be removed and the almighty "I" be exalted to the center of the universe in His place. I know you would like to believe that you are a much nicer guy or gal than that, but according to Scripture, you are not—that is, apart from the influence of the grace of Christ.

Probing the deep and twisted roots of sin, the prophet Isaiah explained the psychological pathology of Lucifer's fall:

"How art thou fallen from heaven, O Lucifer, son of the morning! how art thou cut down to the ground, which didst weaken the nations! For thou hast said in thine heart, I will ascend into heaven, I will exalt my throne above the stars of God: I will sit also upon the mount of the congregation, in the sides of the north: I will ascend above the heights of the clouds; I will be like the most High" (Isaiah 14:12-14).

Notice that the interest of this Scripture is "how" Lucifer fell. By what motive and means and machination did the holy angel, closest to God, vacate his lofty position for a course of rebellion against his Maker? The answer to "the mystery of iniquity" is ever so clear. Lucifer's fall resulted from a desire in his heart to dethrone God and exalt himself in His place. Five times the would-be usurper is quoted as proclaiming the object of his corrupt infatuation: "I . . . I . . . I . . . I . . . I will be like the Most High." Not in character, but in position and power. As insane as it was, Lucifer actually aspired to occupy God's place in the universe. Such is the intoxicating influence of self-absorption.

As was Isaiah, the prophet Ezekiel was given insight into the hidden motive behind Lucifer's fall:

"Thou art the anointed cherub that covereth; and I have set thee so . . . Thou wast perfect in thy ways from the day that thou wast created, till iniquity was found in thee. By the multitude of thy merchandise they have filled the midst of thee with violence, and thou hast sinned . . . Thine heart was lifted up because of thy beauty, thou hast corrupted thy wisdom by reason of thy brightness" (Ezekiel 28:14-17).

While Isaiah pointed out that the underlying motive in Lucifer's rebellion was to exalt self in the place of God, Ezekiel adds that "violence" was present in his plot. Certainly the full intent of his sinister campaign was not apparent to all observers in the beginning stages. He no doubt masqueraded as a benefactor whose only interest was that God treat all with fairness. Only in this guise could he have successfully deceived one third of the angels. But secreted in his heart, beneath the surface of his benevolent countenance, was deception and violence. Jesus explained that Satan's attempt at marshalling support and building a kingdom has been founded on lies covertly concealing murderous intent. Addressing the men who were plotting His crucifixion, He said:

"Ye are of your father the devil, and the lusts [desires] of your father ye will do. He was a murderer from the beginning, and abode not in the truth, because there is no truth in him. When he speaketh a lie, he speaketh of his own: for he is a liar, and the father of it" (John 8:44).

From the beginning of Lucifer's revolt, God understood that murder was behind the lies—the murder of God Himself, that Satan might receive the adoration and praise due to the Creator alone. It seems insane, even ludicrous, for even a lofty angel to suppose he could overthrow God. But sin is not rational. Selfishness is not clear-thinking. It is more than daring; it is suicidal. There may have been flashes of realization in conscience that an attempt to occupy God's place must ultimately end in destruction to himself. But the exhilarating feeling that attends self-exaltation keeps any mind intoxicated as long as it is indulged. Lucifer must have rationalized, *If the lies are convincing enough to amass the support of angels*—his self-crazed heart quivered with excitement—*perhaps I can pull a majority of intelligent beings away from God over to my side. He will have no choice but to yield up the throne.* Yes, it was insane; but such is the nature of sin.

Satan is not alone in his mental-moral illness. In the scripture we have just read, Jesus points out that the murderous motive behind the devil's deceptions also resides in our hearts as fallen human beings: "Ye are of your father the devil, and the [murderous] lusts of your father ye will do." The crucifixion of God in Christ exposed the contents of every human heart. In the murder of Jesus, human beings acted out the end to which self-exaltation tends. Sin demands the death of God in order to build up self on His ruins. In response to the question in the song, "Were you there when they crucified my Lord?" the answer is, *Yes.* I was there, lifting the hammer to drive the nails. I was there, as were you, perfectly represented in the human beings who took the life of the Son of God.

You may be thinking, "No way! I would never have joined with the crowd that hung Him on the cross." But the truth is, in your natural, carnal heart is a deranged psychological makeup so centered on self that you would, if you could, apart from the realizations of His grace, murder your Maker and seat yourself on His throne.

Paul declares of every human heart, including yours and mine, that "the carnal mind is enmity against God" (Romans 8:7). The NIV says, "the sinful mind is hostile to God." And Beck's translation says, "the fleshly mind hates God." If you consider yourself incapable of murder, far less murderous intent toward God, then you don't know yourself or the heinous potential present in your sinfulness. "The heart is deceitful above all things, and desperately wicked: who can know it?" (Jeremiah 17:9).

So deceitful and desperately wicked is the human heart, we have persuaded ourselves that the cross of Christ is a revelation of God lashing out, while evading the truth that it reveals us lashing out at Him. To be sure, there is a biblical sense in which God's wrath is revealed at Calvary. But if we are not careful, we are liable to paint God in dark hues that make Him appear arbitrary and bloodthirsty. The Cross is not a matter of God being so angry about our sin that He must see blood in order to be satisfied.

Christianity, at the heart of which is the substitutionary death of Christ, when rightly understood, stands out clearly distinct from all other world religions. When we allow the Scriptures to speak for themselves, free from human bias, there are significant elements of truth in the concept of substitution. But so rough cut has the biblical truth of substitutionary atonement been presented, that many intelligent minds offhandedly reject Christianity as little different, if different at all, from all the many pagan religions of history.

Nearly every pagan religious system through the ages has contained the element of a divinely required sacrifice. This ingenious move on Satan's part makes his lethal misrepresentation of God look as much like the truth as possible. So common were animal sacrifices in ancient times that the Hebrew nation must have appeared much the same, with its elaborate sacrificial system. When Jesus died on the cross, and the newly formed Christian church declared His death to be a sacrifice, the whole thing could easily be misrepresented as human sacrifice, like those common to paganism. But the message intended by God in the Hebrew sacrificial system, as well as in the cross of Christ, is very distinct from the pagan concept of sacrifice. By capitalizing on the distorted perceptions of God natural to our carnal hearts, Satan has succeeded to a significant degree in blurring that line of distinction.

The core essence of pagan belief is that suffering and death appease the wrath of God; that He is the hostile party in the broken relationship between Himself and fallen human beings. But if we suffer adequately or can inflict sufficient suffering upon an animal or a human in our place, then He will be satisfied and grant His reluctant favor. In this paradigm, a three-party arrangement is evident:

1. The sinner, who has aroused the anger of God.

2. A wrathful God, who needs personal satisfaction that can only be derived from inflicting suffering and imposing death; only then will He even consider letting us off the hook with forgiveness.

3. A third-party victim, who is made to suffer and die as a substitute for the sinner.

There are a number of serious problems with the three-party picture, foremost of which is that it makes no legal or moral sense for an innocent third-party victim to suffer the penalty for the wrongdoer. If such an arrangement could actually satisfy God, then we would be forced to conclude that His law and His wrath are irrational and arbitrary, meaning there is no actual relationship between law and sin and death. If God's wrath can be appeased by venting rage on an innocent third party, then it follows that there is no real problem with sin other than the fact that God doesn't want us doing it: His law is arbitrary. Moreover, since we have failed to meet His arbitrary demands, we had better suffer ourselves or find a whipping boy to suffer in our place: His wrath is arbitrary.

Biblical Christianity proclaims, in extreme contrast to the third-party view of substitution, that God has given Himself as our Substitute, to bear our sin and its inherent, divinely-ordained penalty. Hence there are only two parties involved in the atonement:

1. The sinner, who has aroused in God a painful tension between a holy, rational anger against sin and an equally holy, rational mercy toward the sinner.

2. An infinitely just and infinitely merciful God, who loves us so selflessly that He has chosen to give Himself to suffer and die as our Substitute.

This is why the doctrine of the divinity of Christ is so vital. There are heavy and ugly implications if the One hanging on the cross is anyone less than God Himself. If He was merely a man or even an angel, then God has given virtually nothing and required a sacrifice that in no way resembles selfless love. The universe becomes an extremely dark and foreboding place; love and trust become impossibilities.

But be at peace. Christ was not a mere man suffering to appease the wrath of a selfish, demanding God. No! (As I write this, I'm so happy I could jump to the sky and try to touch Him.) He was, oh glorious reality, God Himself in human flesh, giving . . . giving . . . giving all He could possibly give.

If, then, God was the Giver at the Cross, who required and caused the suffering and death of Christ? Don't we like to say that Jesus endured the anger and punishment of God on the cross? Yes, we do like to say that. Maybe we should stop saying it, unless we're willing to go out of our way to explain what we mean by such language. Do we mean that God the Father somehow inflicted suffering on Christ and then killed Him in order to get something out of His system? Whether that is what we mean or not, many people think that is what we mean. It is clear that the Bible teaches no such thing.

For starters, the Bible does not teach that Christ died on the cross to resolve any kind of *arbitrary* anger in God. Read the entire New Testament and you will not find a single verse that says the Father crucified, killed, tortured, or otherwise inflicted suffering or death on Christ.

Yes, God is angered by sin. To say He hates sin would be an extreme understatement. But why does it anger Him and what is the nature of His anger? When we speak of God as angry and wrathful, it should always be distinguished from the common association of those words with human anger and wrath.

"The wrath of man worketh not the righteousness of God" (James 1:20).

"For a man's anger cannot promote the justice of God" (NEB).

"Human anger does not promote divine righteousness" (Moffatt).

Obviously, there is an infinite difference between human and divine anger. I like what the excellent theologian, John Stott, says on this point:

"God's anger is absolutely pure, and uncontaminated by those elements which render human anger sinful. Human anger is usually arbitrary and uninhibited; divine anger is always principled and controlled. Our anger tends to be a spasmodic outburst, aroused by pique and seeking revenge; God's is a continuous, settled antagonism, aroused only by evil, and expressed in its condemnation. God is entirely free from personal animosity or vindictiveness; indeed, He is sustained simultaneously with undiminished love for the offender. . . . When thinking of the great and living God, it is better to look up than down, and outside than inside ourselves" (*The Cross of Christ*, pp. 105-107).

So what actually happened on that hill far away as the Son of

God hung between heaven and earth? Did Christ bear the wrath of God at Calvary? What part did the Father act in the suffering and death of Christ? A number of Scriptures bear a consistent testimony to answer these questions:

" 'Him [Christ], *being delivered* by the determined purpose and foreknowledge of God, *you have taken* by lawless hands, have crucified, and put to death; whom God raised up, having loosed [destroyed] the pains of death, because it was not possible that He should be held by it' " (Acts 2:23, 24, NKJV).

Notice that in the direct, primary sense, Christ was "put to death" by "lawless hands." What part did God play in the ordeal? He "delivered" Christ over to those lawless hands by which He was "taken"—God the Giver in love, we the takers in selfish hostility. Christ died "by the determined purpose and foreknowledge of God" at our hands. In other words, God allowed what we did in order to accomplish a divine purpose. In His foreknowledge, He knew the murderous nature of our sin. He knew we would lash out at Him, and He determined beforehand to bear our sin with unbroken forgiveness and love. Only thus could we see Him for who He really is and the spell of selfishness be broken.

A New Testament prayer follows the same basic pattern:

" 'Lord, You are God, . . . who by the mouth of Your servant David have said: "Why did the nations rage, and the people plot vain things? The kings of the earth took their stand, and the rulers were gathered together against the Lord and against His Christ." For truly against Your holy Servant Jesus, whom You anointed, both Herod and Pontius Pilate, with the Gentiles and the people of Israel, were gathered together to do whatever Your hand and Your purpose determined before to be done' " (Acts 4:24-28, NKJV).

Three times the word "against" is used to emphasize that what happened at the Cross was done "against the Lord and His Christ," not *by* the Lord *to* Christ. The "rage" of fallen humanity was heaped upon Him; and God permitted it because He discerned a beneficial "purpose" that could only be achieved by submitting to our rage. He who has taught us that "a soft answer turneth away wrath" (Proverbs 15:1), chose the path of silent submission to our anger in order to prove His love and expose sin for what it really is.

Did the Father cause the suffering and death of Christ?

Yes and no!

Yes, if we mean He delivered Him over to suffering and death according to His own wise purpose of grace. Yes, if we mean that the Father gave up His Son to experience the tormenting psychological agony of our guilt.

No, if we mean He acted as an arbitrary source of pain and death, as the tormentor and executioner of His Son. No, if we mean that the Father assumed a position of vicious hostility toward His Son. Christ suffered and died at *our* hands, under the burden of *our* sin, by the gracious, self-sacrificing purpose of the Father.

"Who [Christ], when he was reviled, reviled not again; when he suffered, he threatened not; but committed himself to him that judgeth righteously: Who his own self bare our sins in his own body on the tree, that we, being dead to sins, should live unto righteousness: by whose stripes ye were healed. For ye were as sheep going astray; but are now returned unto the Shepherd and Bishop of your souls" (1 Peter 2:23-25).

In this text, Peter points out that Christ bore our sins by submitting to the reviling and suffering we poured out upon Him.

That self-sacrificing submission on His part, the apostle explains, reacts within those who see and believe it, to effect our healing from sin and move us to "live unto righteousness." Having gone "astray," we are "now," in the light of Calvary's love, "returned" to Him whom we once hated. "For Christ also hath once suffered for sins, the just for the unjust, that he might bring us to God" (1 Peter 3:18). The sufferings of Christ do not bring God to us, as though He needed to be appeased and moved, but rather "bring us to God." He saw nothing at the Cross that caused Him to love us any more than He already did. There was no need for change or movement on God's part. He was already where He needed to be, very much in love with us and eager to receive us when we would wake up to His goodness and love.

The Cross is Jehovah's awakening kiss upon our tight, cold lips, pulsing and warm with life-giving, self-sacrificing love.

So where was the Father when Christ suffered at Calvary?

Smiling and weeping in the paradoxical beauty of mercy and justice! "God was in Christ, reconciling the world unto himself," and yet, God "delivered him up for us all" as Jesus cried out, "My God, my God, why hast thou forsaken me?" (2 Corinthians 5:19; Romans 8:32; Matthew 27:46). Here is the unraveling of the mystery of God's wrath. In holy hatred of sin and unrelenting love for the sinner, the Father handed over His Son to bear the guilt inherent in our sin and to endure the selfish, murderous rage lashing out from our sin. This fits perfectly with Paul's definition of divine wrath. He explains that it is God giving sinners over to receive in themselves the penalty inherent in their sin (Romans 1:18-28). Christ felt "forsaken" by God, "delivered" up to suffer all that sin ultimately is, not pounced upon with hostility.

The Father was right there with His Son all along, behind the darkening veil imposed by our sin, feeling the pain of the agonizing separation.

I can love a God like that. I am so glad He is that kind of God. You can love Him too. I know you can, because your heart, like mine, yearns to love and be loved with such passionate grace.

Father God: To think that my very humanity was present at the Cross, lashing out in rage against You! The truth causes my soul to shudder with self-hatred and sorrow. And yet, You take my vile heart into Your own without hesitation, and then give it back to me cleansed and restored with self-respect. I can feel all my shame and fear washing away as I stand under the tears dripping from Your compassionate countenance. I can't wait to meet You face-to-face! Until then, I will gaze upon Your heart in Christ and find pleasure in what I see. In Christ, I pray. Amen.

9
THE MURDER OF GOD

A scene is presented to my mind just now,
    As on my knees in prayer I bow.
In the darkness of night I see the form of a man,
    As he reaches to heaven with angry hands.
He firmly laid hold of an innocent Lamb,
    Whom now I know as the great I AM.
He wrenched the Lamb from His throne on high,
    To the darkness below, I began to cry.

The horrible man then smote my Lord,
    And bound His hands tight with cord.
He tied Him to a post of wood,
    Where wicked men and demons stood.

They laughed and mocked at the man then bound,
    The God of heaven up off the ground.
The wicked man then raised his whip,
    My Savior's flesh to tear and rip.

He raised his arm, and with great might,
He thrashed the God of life and light.
Thirty-nine times, so cruel was He beat,
Mangled and torn from His head to His feet.

The fiendish man then cut the cord,
And I watched my Savior fall.
Now more terrible than before
Were the vivid scenes I saw.

He laid my Lord on a rough old cross,
The symbol of satanic rite.
The Savior as a quiet Lamb,
Made no struggle, nor offered fight.

He drove large spikes of sharpened steel,
Through His hands and feet with devilish zeal.
I wondered with awe that such evil could be,
I hid my eyes that I might not see.

As I heard wicked men and demons mock,
I could hardly bear the sound.
The man did thrust the cross with force
To a hole dug in the ground.
I heard a thud,
And the sound of ripping flesh;
The echo is upon my ear still fresh.

Wonder, O heavens;
>   Be astonished, ye worlds far and nigh!
Groan all creation,
>   For your Maker now dies!

Satisfied with his hellish work,
>   The man then turned away.
"Now," said he, "I may go on unhindered
>   In my own selfish way."

I cried out in anguish the following words,
>   It seemed my question everyone heard:
Who is this man so hateful and cruel,
>   O who could be so vile as he,
To pull God from His throne on high,
>   And hang Him on a tree?

Then, behold!
>   Thunder through the whole earth crashed,
>   And in the darkness lightning flashed.

And as these bolts did lighten the sky,
>   O horrible reality, his face I see,
>   That wicked man, it's me, it's me!
>   I drove the nails at Calvary.
>   The truth, at last, I finally see.

O God of heaven, hear my prayer,
    My guilt, O Lord, I cannot bear.
Forgive my murderous, evil work,
    I'm sorry for your pain and hurt.

Cleanse, O cleanse my hostile mind,
    The way of life, help me to find.
Hear the prayer of Jesus, the Faithful and True,
    "Father forgive them,
        for they know not what they do."

Just as surely as this man is me,
    Know, O sinner, that this man is thee.
Are you truly repentant and sorry for sin?
    Or if haply you could, would you slay Him again?

Please for the sake of Jesus the Christ,
    Cease to do evil and learn to do right.
Follow this Man as One dying for sin,
    That through His death you might live again.

He loves you, O man, dear woman and youth,
    Will you bow at His feet
        and acknowledge the truth?
That we are this man, it was you and I,
    That by our sin God was crucified.

Only acknowledge your sin, your guilt and woe;
    Receive His pardon, and you will know,
That you are His child, redeemed from sin,
    Never to wander or rebel again. Amen.

10
BLISS BEYOND THE DOOR

NOT LONG AGO I read about an extremely disappointing honey-moon. If you were to ask Ruben about it, he'd say it was lousy. Ask Fiona and she'll tell you that lousy is an understatement. "It was horrible!" she would say.

Their courtship was flawless, to hear them talk of it. The wedding was perfect. And the honeymoon was supposed to be heaven on earth. Fiona's father reserved for the lovebirds the very best penthouse suite in their city. One night cost $3000!

With an excitement only known to virgin love, the two of them drove away from the lingering reception to the place prepared for them. They arrived at the hotel after midnight. Up the elevator they went, passing one mediocre floor after another, until they were at the top. If the elegance of the hallway was any indication of the suite, it was going to be beyond their expectations.

Ruben inserted the key in the door, looking back at Fiona with a lovesick smile. Carrying her across the threshold, he nearly dropped her, and she nearly sat up in his arms, as they saw the room. They were shocked. It was hardly much bigger than the elevator. The furnishings were nice, but minimal: a beautiful sofa, which turned out to be a hide-a-bed and a small table with two chairs and a silk plant. The small bathroom didn't even have a shower.

Fiona began to cry.

Ruben was furious.

"I can't believe they think this is a honeymoon suite," Fiona mumbled through her tears. "I'm going to demand a refund!"

But it was late and they were tired. So they figured they had better make their complaint in the morning. Pulling out the hide-a-bed, they tried to get some rest. The next day, as they stepped out of the elevator in the lobby, the manager greeted them with a smile: "How are the newlyweds, and how was your stay?"

"Quite frankly," Ruben retorted, "we're fried and our stay was totally miserable."

Fiona expressed her bitter disappointment and requested a refund to be made to her father immediately.

"I don't understand," the manager questioned, "this is the very best honeymoon suite in the city, perhaps in the entire state."

"If that's your best, I'd hate to see your worst," Fiona complained. "Motel 6 would have been better. At least there you don't have to sleep on a hide-a-bed."

"Oh, I see," the manager turned solemn. "I know what has happened. Please come with me and I'll explain."

Up they went in the elevator to the top floor. The hotel manager escorted the unhappy couple to the same door they had approached with such excitement the night before. They all stepped into the tiny room and the manager pointed to a door and said, "Didn't you ever open that door?"

"That door?" Ruben questioned with a sick feeling developing in his stomach. "I thought it was just a closet."

"No, that is not a closet, sir," the manager replied, shaking his head with a sigh. "Please open the door and take a look inside."

As Ruben flung the door open, he and Fiona were amazed and deflated at what they saw. The large room was the size of a house. The entire back wall was comprised of a series of picture windows overlooking the city. There was an indoor pool and a bubbling Jacuzzi, a beautiful table set with more gourmet food than two people could eat in a week, a surround-sound stereo system, and a large bed centered on top of a pedestal to be ascended by five stairs.

"The small room in which you spent the night," the manager explained, "is the foyer for receiving room service and guests. Only the honeymooners actually enter the suite itself during their stay."

"Oh, how I wish we had opened that door," Fiona cried.

I'd like to invite you to open that door, dear reader, to move beyond the foyer in your spiritual experience and enter into a deeper intimacy with God. Many Christians mistakenly assume that the receiving room is the honeymoon suite. They become dwarfed in the childish perceptions of spirituality—"(Touch not; taste not; handle not)" (Colossians 2:21). And all the while there is bliss beyond the door.

I want to invite you to move beyond cultural Christianity—hanging around in the foyer because you were born and raised in the church.

Beyond formal religion—hanging around in the foyer because being slightly religious makes you feel like you'll make it to heaven.

Beyond intellectual spirituality—hanging around in the foyer because being theologically correct feeds your pride.

Beyond the place of legal, obligatory connection with God—hanging around in the foyer because of a sense of raw duty to do what is right.

I want to invite you into the inner chamber of genuine, heart-felt, radical, sold-out, intimate love relationship with God. If you choose to accept the invitation, there is only one door of entrance. The door of cultural religion won't lead there. Nor will the door of formalism, or intellectualism, or obligation. There is only one passageway into the heart of God. That door is Christ (John 10:9). More specifically, that door is opened in the soul when the inner eye of faith encounters the self-sacrificing love of God displayed in Christ at the Cross.

Come with me to the elevator, and I'll escort you to the door.

The ancient Hebrew people considered all the Old Testament to be holy. But there was one book they regarded as more sacred than all the others. They referred to this book as the *Most Holy Place* of Scripture, an allusion to the second room of the sanctuary in which resided the personal presence of the Almighty One.

The one book regarded as Most Holy was not Genesis, with its glorious account of Creation. Nor was it Exodus, with its record of God's holy law. Nor Leviticus with its detailed instructions for conducting the sacrificial services of the temple. It wasn't even any of the distinctly prophetic books pointing forward to the Messiah, such as Daniel or Isaiah.

The Most Holy portion of Scripture for the ancient Jews was the Song of Solomon.

Are you surprised?

I don't blame you. I mean, come on, the Song of Solomon? It's just a passionate song portraying the romantic exchanges between a man and a woman who are "lovesick" (Song of Solomon 2:4, NKJV). We *are* surprised. We don't get it. That is, until we remember something we are so very prone to forget—that this God with whom we have to do; this God so lofty and high above us; this God who created the universe with words; this God who shook Mt. Sinai as He gave His law; this God whom we fear more than love and avoid more than pursue; this God whom we talk about more than we talk to; this God is, after all, a person. A person above all other persons, no doubt, but a person, nonetheless. A person with a mind and emotions. A person who loves and longs to be loved. He is not a mass of cosmic energy. He is not an impersonal force. He is not a distant dictator. No! God is a person, the most largehearted, sensitive Person in all the universe. And ultimately what He desires is heart-to-heart intimacy with you and me.

When we remember this, then it makes perfect sense that the Song of Solomon very well could be the Most Holy Place of Scripture, for this love poem portrays the most intimate human relationship we experience. The Song of Solomon is so intimate in its description of romantic love that we nearly blush to read it. But the fact that it is included as a part of God's Holy Word indicates at least two things:

1. God approves of, even encourages, extremely passionate love between a man and a woman within the protective sanctum of marriage.

2. Such love symbolically communicates God's desire for an intimate spiritual relationship with each of His children.

Regarding the first point, I would not recommend that men use Solomon's approach to charm. You'll want to update your language. Some of the things Solomon said to his lover should never be said to a modern woman:

"You remind me of my horse" (1:9).

"Your hair is like a flock of goats" (4:1).

"Your teeth are like shaved sheep, just washed" [no doubt meaning they were brushed and flossed] (4:2).

"Your neck is like an armory tower" (4:4).

"Your belly button is like a goblet" (7:2).

"Your waist is like a heap of wheat" (7:2).

"Your nose is like the tower of Lebanon" (7:4).

"Your head is like a mountain" (7:5; some of these are slightly paraphrased for clarity).

Regarding the second point, reading some Bible versions, such as the King James, leaves the impression that the Song of Solomon makes no mention at all of God, and therefore has no spiritual point.

Not true.

God is brought to view one time in the poem, and that at its climactic, crescendo point. After describing with great detail the passionate love between a man and a woman, Solomon makes the parallel to God. First notice the King James Version. Try to pick out the word that should have been translated *God:*

"Set me as a seal upon thine heart, as a seal upon thine arm: for love is strong as death; jealousy is cruel as the grave: the coals thereof are coals of fire, which hath a most vehement flame. Many waters cannot quench love, neither can the floods drown it: if a man would give all the substance of his house for love, it would utterly be contemned [condemned]" (Song of Solomon 8:6, 7).

The word here translated "vehement" is the Hebrew word *Yahh* or *Jah,* which is the name of God. It appears as *iah* at the end of human names, such as Isaiah, which means "Jehovah will see"; or Jeremiah, which means "Jehovah will rise."

Notice the rendering now in one of the more modern Bible versions:

"Set me like a seal on your heart, like a seal on your arm. For love is strong as Death, jealousy as relentless as Sheol. The flash of it is a flash of fire, a flame of Yahweh Himself" (The Jerusalem Bible).

Follow the pattern of the poem to catch Solomon's deep spiritual point.

1. Love is "strong." How strong? "Strong as Death." In other words, love does not back up or diminish in the face of losing self in death. The jealousy of love is as unrelenting as the grave. As firmly as a dead person is bound to the grave, just so tightly does love hold the subjects of its passion.

2. Then Solomon draws a parallel between love and fire. Not just fire as such, but the very fire of God Himself. The characteristic of fire which Solomon has in mind is brought out in the next verse: "Many waters cannot quench love." He wants us to understand that God's love is like an unquenchable fire.

But why fire?

When Moses reminded Israel of when God gave them His holy law, he said of the Lord, "He shined . . . from his right hand went a fiery law for them. Yea, he loved the people"

(Deuteronomy 33:2, 3). "And the sight of the glory of the Lord was like devouring fire on the top of the mount in the eyes of the children of Israel" (Exodus 24:17). "For the Lord thy God is a consuming fire" (Deuteronomy 4:24). Paul made the same kind of parallel between God and fire: "Our God is a consuming fire" (Hebrews 12:29).

We are not to conclude from such texts that God is composed in nature of literal fire. But rather, as Moses said, His glory is "*like* devouring fire . . . in the eyes" of human beings. God's law is fiery; His glory is like a devouring fire; and His love is like an unquenchable fire. In what sense? In that the righteousness of God's character of love stands in distinct contrast to our sinful selfishness. The use of the words *consuming* and *devouring* indicate the reality that God's righteous love not only exposes sin, it destroys it like darkness vanishes before the greater power of light. God's love is wholly incompatible with sin. Whenever the two meet in close proximity, the lesser is consumed by the greater. With unrelenting passion, love devours all that is sinful and selfish. To sin, wherever found, God is a consuming fire by virtue of who and what He is in character.

It is for this very reason that God has hidden Himself behind the subduing veil that is Christ. In Jesus we see the sunlight, as it were, without looking directly into the sun; we see the attractive beauty of God's character in bearable splendor, without having to face the full brilliance of divine glory before we can survive it. As we come to know God in Christ, the heat of His glorious love is slowly turned up to consume away our sin with merciful, healing gentleness. As we see Him more and more clearly, we see ourselves in ugly contrast with progressive clarity as well. With each sensitizing revelation we have the opportunity to dive deeper into the flame, to be "washed . . . by the spirit [the mental process] of judgment [discernment] and by the spirit of burning" (Isaiah 4:4, NKJV). "The path of the just is like the shining sun, that shines ever brighter unto the perfect day" (Proverbs 4:18, NKJV). " 'For He is like a refiner's fire and like launderer's soap' " (Malachi 3:2, NKJV).

Christianity is intended to be an ever-deepening journey into the heart of God, by which the beholding of His glory gradually transforms the believer into the same character likeness (2 Corinthians 3:18). For those who persist in sin to the ruin of their inner capacity to discern and reflect God's love, that fire of divine love which would have cleansed them will, on the day of final reckoning, ignite in their souls a destructive measure of shame and guilt. The glory of Him who is love will be more than the conscience can bear. On the day of unveiled encounter, they will experience psychological and emotional meltdown in God's immediate presence. " 'For behold, the day is coming, burning like an oven, and all the proud, yes, all who do wickedly will be stubble. And the day which is coming shall burn them up,' says the Lord of hosts, 'That will leave them neither root nor branch. But to you who fear My name [love My character] the Sun of Righteousness shall arise with healing in His wings [in the rays of light that emanate from Him]' " (Malachi 4:1, 2, NKJV). Everyone will eventually meet God in all the radiance of His glorious love. Some will be consumed, while others are healed by the very same encounter.

The love of which Solomon speaks—strong as death, relentless as the grave, and as unquenchable as the fire of God's glory— was manifested in Christ. At Gethsemane and Calvary we behold

God's love put to the severest test and emerging from the fire victorious over the law of sin and death. In a word, the sufferings of Jesus consisted of a raw encounter with *reality*. He entered into the uncharted realm of total truth, both about God and about fallen mankind. He experienced perfect consciousness of God's holy love in contrast to our sinful selfishness. In His mind and heart He faced, with painfully acuity, the full reality of human wickedness being consumed by the holiness of God. When the two realities reached their zenith point in His conscience, they clashed for the mastery, and God's love was victorious. He chose to resist "the law of sin and death" and to keep tight hold of the principle of selfless love. Sinful humanity died in the death of Christ and an entirely new humanity emerged triumphant over sin and drenched in the blood of relentless love.

The prophet Isaiah explains:

"As a result of the anguish of His soul, He will see it and be satisfied; by His knowledge the Righteous One, My Servant, will justify the many, as He will bear their iniquities . . . because He poured out Himself to death" (Isaiah 53:11, 12, NASB).

The American Standard Version gives this added flavor:

"By the knowledge of Himself shall My righteous Servant justify many; and He shall bear their iniquities."

The catalyst, or igniting factor, for the sufferings of Christ was "His knowledge," His first-hand, experiential knowledge. Of what? Of "Himself" as God and of fallen mankind as He bore our sins. The two chief characteristics of the Savior's life and death were that (1) He knew God fully as the Son of God, and (2) He knew humanity fully as the Son of Man. "He knew all men, and needed not that any should testify of man: for he knew what was in man"

(John 2:24, 25). " 'Nor does anyone know the Father except the Son' " (Matthew 11:27, NKJV).

Christ knew what was in man by virtue of the fact that "God sent forth his Son, made of a woman, made under the law, to redeem them that were under the law" (Galatians 4:4, 5). "Forasmuch then as the children are partakers of flesh and blood, he also himself likewise took part of the same; that through death he might destroy him that had the power of death, that is, the devil" (Hebrews 2:14). He died our death, the death of sin and guilt, by experiential knowledge. By entering into our fallen humanity, under the workings of the law of sin and death, Jesus tasted "death for every man" (Hebrews 2:9). "He was numbered with the transgressors" (Isaiah 53:12). He knew God by virtue of the fact that He was the divine Son of the Father. He was a perfect partaker of the divine character of selfless, righteous love. God's intense, holy hatred of sin and His equally intense love for sinners were vividly clear in the mind of Jesus.

Christ achieved our salvation "by His knowledge" of both God and sinful humanity. This was the lethal formula that trembled in the Savior's hands as He prayed, "O My Father, if it be possible, let this cup pass from me: nevertheless, not as I will, but as thou wilt" (Matthew 26:39). He experienced the full magnitude of our guilt as He voluntarily made His sinless "soul an offering for sin" (Isaiah 53:10). Upon entering the Garden of Gethsemane, He entered the dark psychological reality of sin's unbuffered torment. Divulging the mystery of His anguish, He told the disciples, "My soul is exceeding sorrowful, even unto death" (Matthew 26:38). No physical cause for death is here present. No nails through His hands. No crown of thorns on His head. No spear thrust into His side. And yet, He is dying deep in His holy, sin-laden heart. Our sin rolled heavily upon His conscience, as though it were His own.

As the Savior finally hung between heaven and earth upon the cross, He cried out in soul-agony, "My God, My God, why hast thou forsaken me?" (Matthew 27:46). He felt the separation which sin makes between God and guilty man. For a period of time He could not see through the thick cloud of our shame bearing down upon Him. It seemed as though our sin was more than God could forgive, as though it was powerful enough to make God cease loving us. But as He continued to suffer under our guilt, He continued to feel the love of the Father reaching out through Him into our sinfulness. By His knowledge of the Father's character, He penetrated through the separating veil of darkness. By faith He regained a clear sense of God's enormous love for sinners no matter how ugly our sin.

Beautiful conquest!

As He closed His eyes with a final sigh of peaceful trust, the love of God had proved itself "strong as death and unrelenting as the grave," unwilling to give us up even in the face of complete self-sacrifice. The unquenchable flame had consumed our sin upon the altar of His enlightened heart.

Holy Father: Your love is so much greater than my feeble mind can grasp. If a person were to give all the substance of his house for such love, it would be utterly scorned as a ridiculous offer. Nothing this world has to give its prisoners can be compared in any degree to the value of Your love. To know it, to drink it in, to be cleansed by it, and to reflect it back to You is my most ardent desire. Strengthen me to let its fire burn deep and eternal in my heart. With my eyes on Christ, I pray. Amen.

11
WORDS OF LIGHT IN THE DARK

WORDS. THEY ARE SO POWERFUL. God creates with them physical matter out of nothing and spiritual beauty out of human sinfulness. For those who know well the story of Jesus, one word will paint an entire scene and evoke a heart full of emotion. A chronological construction of key words will move the mind through every scene in the story, while allowing for the Holy Spirit to employ the imagination without the obstruction imposed by too many words. Walk with me through a gallery of words, pausing and pondering where needed, as we reconstruct the Savior's passion as it unfolded in a garden and on a hill not so long ago.

Nightfall. Moon. Stars. Men walking. Eleven. Not twelve. Stopping. Garden. Four. Walking. Heavy. Wondering. "My soul!" Sorrow. Dying. "Pray!" Drowsiness. Slumber. One. Alone. Lonely.
Staggering. Burden. Invisible. Internal. Falling. Prostrate. Agony. Weeping. Sweating. Bleeding. Pleading. Cup? Cup! Trem-

bling. Struggling. Weighing. "Me?" "Them?" "Resurrection?" Grappling. "Me?" "Them?" Choosing. "Them?" "Yes!" "Them!" Dying. Angel. Comfort. Strength.

Mob. Torches. Betrayer. "Master!" Kiss. Betrayal. "Friend." "Why?" Flash. Glory. Powerful. Falling. Confusion. Free. Arising. Composure. "Who?" "Jesus!" Submissive. Grabbing. Sword. Slash. Blood. Ear. Reproof. Touch. Healing. Fear. Self-preservation. Fleeing! Abandonment. Alone again. Surrounded. Alone. Heldfast. Alone still!

Midnight. Darkness. Trial. High Priest. Religion without God. Expediency. Pride. Witnesses. Witnesses? Liars! Question. "Christ?" Silence. Question. Swearing. Answer. Unacceptable. Indignation. Spitting. Striking. Anger. Threats. Accusation. "Blasphemy!" "Guilty!" Guilty? Innocent!

Fire. Watching. Listening. Identified. Question. Denial. Question. Denial. Question. Cursing. Denial. Rooster. Crowing. Recall. Glance. Disappointment. Compassion. Shame. Weeping. Fleeing.

Betrayer. Realization. Conviction. Remorse. Shame. Silver. Value? None! Desperation. Confession. "Stop!" "Never!" Hardness. Coldness. Run. Rope. Neck. Suicide.

Blindfolded. Mockery. Punch. "Who?" "Prophesy!" Laughter. Morning. Bound. Walking. Pilate. Judgment. Trial. Accusations. Standing. Examination. Question. Answer. Conviction. Discernment. "Innocent!" Galilee. Galilaean? "Ah!" "Herod!" Sent. Questions. Silence. "Pilate!" Returned.

Compromise? Release? "One!" "Who?" "Barabbas!" The Innocent? The guilty? Choose? The Guilty!

Soldiers. Brutality. Stripped. Tied. Leather. Bone. Metal. Sharp.

Handle. Arm. Scourging. Lifting. Falling. Whipping. Tearing. Whipping. Tearing. Whipping. Tearing. Hanging. Bleeding. Dignity. Silence. Clothed. Scarlet robe. Crown. Thorns. Scepter. Mockery. "Hail!" "King!" Spit. "Good enough?" "No!" "Innocent!" "No!" Manipulation. Pressure. Basin. Hands. Washed. "Crucify!" Cross. "Walk!" Heavy. Dragging. Staggering. Falling. Rising. Falling. Rising. Falling. "You!" Relief. Hill. Climb. Fall. Climb.

Wood. Nails. Hammer. Grabbing. Pushing. Holding. (No need!) Submission. Silence. Pounding. Penetrating. Tearing. Twitching. Jerking. Quivering. Shaking. Bleeding. Loving. Still! Observers. "Why?" Confusion. Tears. Fear.

Lift. Balance. Hole. Thud. Rip. Gouge. Hanging. Breathless. Gasping. Eyes rounded. Writhing. Agony. Looking down. Eye contact. Looking out. Eye contact. Tears. Lifting. Wrenching. Dropping. Pausing. Lifting. Wrenching. Dropping. Weight. Hands. Feet. Holes. Gaping. Vinegar. Refusal.

Cross. Crosses. Right. Left. Words. Reviling. "Save Self!" "Us!" Reproof. Discerning. Acknowledging. Asking. Paradise. "Remember me?" Acceptance. Promise. Gratitude. Peace. Mother. Alone. Concern. "Son!" Please. "Mother!" Earthquake.

Forsaken? "Father?" "Why?"

Sky. Sun. Eclipse. Moon. Darkness.

Soul. Pain. Eclipse. Love. Light.

Unrelenting. Holding. Continuing. "Forgive!"

Dying. Loving. Selfless. Triumphant.

Demons. Trembling. Realizing. Defeat.

Peace. Submission. Trust. Eyes shut.

Darkness. Darkness? No. Light!

Experiential Grace: Transforming Believers

12
THE PSYCHOLOGY
OF GRACE

I STEP THROUGH a familiar door, take a look around, and what I
see causes me to shout above all the noisy activity, "What exactly
is going on in here?"

That is, in my mind.

Sometimes when I try to understand what's going on inside
of me, the task seems overwhelming. No doubt you identify. My
heart resonates with King David as he exclaimed to the Lord,
"Thank you for making me so wonderfully complex! It is amazing to think about. Your workmanship is marvelous" (Psalm
139:14, The Living Bible).

Yes, it is marvelous, and I am thankful, but complex is also
an appropriate word. And things upstairs have been made sig-
nificantly more complex due to the psychological derangements
imposed upon us by sin. God made us beautifully complex—a
finely tuned psycho-emotional machine of balance and harmony.
But sin has added to the beauty a perverse complexity. There

are things going on in our heads that shouldn't be.

We Christians often refer to Jesus as "the Great Physician," no doubt an allusion to the many physical healings He performed. It's a fine title. But He deserves another title as well, even more so. He healed far more hearts than bodies. Maybe we should call Him the Great Psychiatrist. Physical disease is almost no problem at all in comparison to our mental illness as human beings.

The sin problem began in a mind—the mind of Lucifer: "For thou hast said *in thine heart*, I . . . I . . . I . . . I . . . I . . ." (Isaiah 14:13, 14). Of the fallen one, Ezekiel said, "Iniquity was found *in thee;*" you have "filled *the midst of thee* with violence, . . . Thine *heart* was lifted up because of thy beauty, . . . Thou hast defiled *thy sanctuaries* [the temple of the mind]" (Ezekiel 28:15-18).

The prophet Isaiah described the human condition of sin as mental illness:

"The whole head is sick, and the whole heart faint. From the sole of the foot even unto the head there is no soundness in it; but wounds, and bruises, and putrifying sores" (Isaiah 1:5, 6).

Loosely translated, we humans are sick in the head, mentally ill, emotionally dysfunctional, spiritually deranged. Sin is a heart problem. And salvation is all about heart healing, as we are about to discover.

Man is mind. We have bodies, but we are minds, with all that includes—intellect, conscience, memory, reason, imagination, volition, motive, emotion, etc. Paul called this dimension of our humanity "the inner man" (Ephesians 3:16). Jesus called it " 'the inside,' " in contrast to " 'the outside' " (Matthew 23:25, 26, NKJV). It is here, on the inside, that each person's identity and character reside. Allow me to give a rather crude illustration to demonstrate that your body is simply the instrument, as it were, of your mind.

If on Sunday you had a kidney transplant, you would still be the same person you were before another person's physical organ was put into your body.

Agreed?

If on Monday you had a heart transplant, you'd still be the same person, though now you have someone else's heart. If on Tuesday you had both hands amputated and two new ones from a fresh cadaver were surgically grafted onto your wrists (two such hand-graft surgeries have been performed to date), you'd still be you and not the other person, although it would take some getting used to seeing someone else's scars and calluses on your new hands.

The list of transplants could go on, but you're tired of surgery so we will stop here. The point is, no matter how many body parts you might lose, and no matter how many body parts from others might be attached to your body, you would still be the same person you always had been. Even if it were possible for you to have a complete body transplant on Wednesday, excluding your brain—in which the wonderful mystery of mind is contained—you would still be the same person on Thursday. In fact, something like a complete body transplant is going to happen to you someday. When you die, your present body will decompose in the ground. On resurrection morning you will be brought to life with a new, immortal body, composed of entirely different particles of matter. And yet, you will still be exactly the same person you were before death. This is because your essential identity is composed of character: thoughts and feelings and motives and memories of the deeds done in the body as expressions of the inner person. The body is, as it were, the house in which you live. Actions of the body are performed at the dictates of the mind. "For as he thinketh in his heart, so is he" (Proverbs 23:7). In other words, the contents of a person's mind determine the way he or she behaves with the body. "Keep thy heart with all diligence; for out of it are the issues of life" (Proverbs 4:23).

Don't misunderstand. The body is vitally significant, so much so that conscious life is impossible without it. But the body merely acts out the dictates of the mind, and is, therefore, the lesser part of who you are. Remaking our body will be a relatively simple matter. At the second coming of Christ, He will, "in a moment, in the twinkling of an eye," as it were, "change our vile body, that it may be fashioned like unto his glorious body" (1 Corinthians 15:52; Philippians 3:21). But the remaking of our minds and emotions is a more difficult and fragile task, even for the Almighty. With the recreating of our body, He is simply dealing with physical matter. A momentary act. But with the recreating of our inner person, He is up against a free will bent on self-serving under the influence of a blinding delusion. He must speak and speak and speak, not a single word of instantaneous material creation, but many words of incremental psycho-spiritual creation, "from glory to glory." Words of self-disclosure in the dark. Words of healing to the unconsciously sick. Words of painful truth to hearts hiding behind lies.

The fall of mankind involved four basic areas of decline. I will list each area according to the order in which Adam and Eve were impacted.

1. *Misperception.* The sin problem entered the human heart on the level of perception. Satan communicated a false picture of

God. He portrayed the Creator as an untrustworthy, self-serving tyrant who was holding Adam and Eve under an unnecessary control (Genesis 3:1-5). While claiming that God was selfish, the tempter sought to subtly arouse selfishness in the human heart, and succeeded. By believing the devil's misrepresentation of God, Eve recorded the false picture in her now-darkened imagination as though it were true. She was deceived by allowing her perception of God to become distorted.

2. *Mistrust.* Once the false picture was believed, trust was broken. Eve ceased to believe that God loved her with selfless interest. She no longer trusted her Maker and chose to live for herself.

3. *Disobedience.* To act in rebellion was the logical next step. Eve's behavioral violation of God's will proceeded out of the problem that had developed in her mind and heart. Outward disobedience is symptomatic of a deep inner fall in the areas of perception and trust.

4. *Guilt.* As soon as the inner rebellion was acted out in disobedience, a sense of condemnation and shame began to weigh heavily upon the conscience. "The eyes of them both were opened, and they knew that they were naked" (Genesis 3:7). Because the sin was entered into with a deceived heart concerning the character of God, the guilt that followed became the vehicle for the deception to continue and deepen. Adam and Eve chose to turn from their Maker and live for self because they believed a distorted picture of Him. Now, as they felt the agonizing pain of guilt for their wrong, their darkened imaginations naturally assumed that the condemnation that pounded upon them must be from God, that the One who was selfishly holding them under His arbitrary control was now imposing upon them an equally arbitrary condemnation. Hence they

were now "afraid" of the very One whom they had always approached without fear, and they sought to hide from Him (Genesis 3:8-10). Their guilt perpetuated the misperception upon which their rebellion was founded. A lethal cycle was set into motion within them.

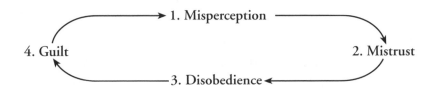

We most often try to resolve the sin problem in ourselves, and in others, by trying to correct outward behavior (a focus on level 3). To be sure, disobedience to God is a serious problem that must be corrected. But the fact is, it cannot be corrected by trying to overcome the wrong behavior while allowing the internal dimension of the sin problem to go on unremedied. Trying to overcome sin by focusing on the sinful behavior is like trying to walk a tight rope by staring intently at your feet and the rope. It is impossible. Only as you look up away from your feet can balance be achieved. Likewise, only as you look up away from yourself to the truth about God can sin be overcome (finding clarity and resolve at level 1). Even if a high level of behavioral discipline is achieved, as long as serious misperceptions of God's character continue, the moral structure is built on a motivational foundation of guilt and fear. The motive for obedience remains self-centered and is, in actuality, disobedience masquerading as obedience. Victory over sin is not really achieved, but rather rebellion continues under the guise of religion. Such is always the case whenever we try to serve God without really loving Him for who He is in character. It is a blind obedience.

The way in which God approached Adam and Eve after their fall is extremely enlightening. It opens our understanding to the beauty of His grace-full character.

"And the Lord God called unto Adam, and said unto him, Where art thou? And he said, I heard thy voice in the garden, and I was afraid, because I was naked; and I hid myself. And he said, Who told thee that thou wast naked? Hast thou eaten of the tree, whereof I commanded thee that thou shouldest not eat?" (Genesis 3:9-11).

Why is an omniscient God asking questions? Is He probing for information He lacks? Is He expecting Adam to tell Him something He doesn't already know? Obviously not. He is asking questions as a means of communicating, not to gain knowledge. He wants Adam and Eve to think about what they have done and to see Him as He is.

The first question is, "Where are you?" God knew exactly where they were and could have pounced upon them without notice, and they knew it. Hiding from Almighty God was an act of phobic insanity. He asked where they were because He wanted them to hear His voice, for much may be communicated in voice tone. It is clear that His call was free from threat and condemnation, by the simple fact that they immediately came out of their hiding place and presented themselves before Him. His call was a compassionate plea intended to communicate, "I'm here, and I know what you've done, and I still love you. Come to Me and I will help you through this tragic situation."

The second question is even more amazing. When Adam explained that they hid in fear because they were naked, God asked, "Who told thee that thou wast naked?"

What an incredible God!

He could have said, "That's right, rebel pair, you are naked; your innocence is stripped away. You had better be afraid, because your guilt is great." But He didn't. The implication in this question is clear. God wanted them to know that He was not the source of their shame and guilt. The message in the question is, "Who called your attention to your nakedness? Not I." Yes, they were naked, guilty of sin, but God had not told them they were guilty. He didn't need to. The realization arose from within their own hearts. And rightly so. What they had done was wrong, and they knew it, painfully so. But God was eager to draw a distinction between the condemnation they felt toward themselves and how He felt toward them. He immediately began explaining the good news of salvation without one word of scorn (3:12-15).

The third question was intended to call added attention to the fact that the guilt they felt was directly derived from their sin: "Hast thou eaten of the tree, whereof I commanded thee that thou shouldest not eat?" The Lord knew they had eaten the forbidden fruit. But He pointed to the sin itself, while refraining from imposing arbitrary condemnation on them, so they could realize that there is something fundamentally wrong with what they had done, and that He loved them still. Are we then to conclude that God does not condemn? Not at all. God does condemn. He condemns sin, while simultaneously loving the sinner.

In this entire interaction between God and the fallen Adam and Eve we are witnessing the Healer of hearts applying His restoring balm of grace. We are watching the Great Psychiatrist in action. Here is revealed the psychology of grace—what it is and how it works. The guilt of sin is shown to be a destructive force, and God's non-condemnatory love is shown to be the healing remedy. Moving forward in time, the apostle Paul captured the essence of how grace operates:

"Where sin abounded, grace did much more abound" (Romans 5:20).

The idea here is of two opposing powers measuring strength and the one surpassing the other. Allow the concept to expand as you read the following translations:

"Though sin is shown to be wide and deep, thank God His grace is wider and deeper still!" (Phillips).

"But where sin was thus multiplied, grace immeasurably exceeded it" (NEB).

"Where sin increased, grace increased all the more" (NIV).

"Sin increased, but grace surpassed it by far" (Moffatt).

"But, where sins were multiplied, the loving-kindness of God was lavished all the more" (The Twentieth Century New Testament).

Grace saves by continuing, continuing, continuing to love to the absolute nth degree. It supercedes guilt as a dominate force. As the law of speed transcends the law of gravity, so the principle of grace transcends the principle of sin. Whereas guilt says, "You are a worthless, rebellious, degraded wretch, undeserving of even one more breath of life." Grace says, "True, so very true, but God loves you still and sees so much value in you that He literally laid down His own life so you may live."

Many people have the idea that God's grace only goes so far

and then has a ceasing point. If a person plunges too deep into sin, so the concept goes, God's wrath picks up where His forgiveness ends. Nothing could be further from the truth. God's pardoning love knows no boundary at all, which is what makes it so extremely powerful. Of Himself the Lord declares, "I am the Lord, I change not" (Malachi 3:6). He is "the same yesterday, and to-day, and forever" (Hebrews 13:8). "With whom is no variableness, neither shadow of turning" (James 1:17). There is no such thing as a sin so bad that God refuses to forgive.

How, then, could anyone ever be lost?

Never because there was a boundary beyond which God's grace would not go! But it is possible for a person to destroy their psychological capacity to be forgiven. In counseling sessions, people sometimes explain their bleak situations and then ask if they may have committed "the unpardonable sin." They inquire, "Will God forgive me, after what I have done?" The answer is always, "Yes!" The real question is, "Can you receive God's forgiveness?" He is always forgiving. Those who are ultimately lost will be lost because they became unforgivable from their own perspective, not God's; that is, they will have become incapable of seeing and embracing God's forgiveness by their own persistent continuance in sin. As long as a person is asking questions like, "Have I committed the unpardonable sin?" they have not. Their concern reveals a significant degree of longing for pardon alive in the conscience.

God's forgiving love is a continual, maximum-brilliance reality of endless, encompassing proportions. But sin is a guilt-imposing force, the chief aim of which is to block our perception of God's merciful love. Grace operates as an overriding force, breaking through the barrier of our guilt and bathing the mind and emotions in the truth of God's sin-transcending love. Grace persuades us that, despite our sins, God continues to place infinite value upon us, revealed by the sacrifice of His own life for our redemption. "Where sin abounded, grace did much more abound."

The apostle John set forth the psychology of grace with these insightful words:

"By this we know love, because He laid down His life for us . . . For if our heart condemns us, God is greater than our heart, and knows all things" (1 John 3:16, 20, NKJV).

John points out that condemnation is a psychological phenomenon that occurs in the human heart because of sin. Condemnation is not arbitrary, but organic to transgression of God's holy law. Far from assuming a posture of condemnation toward the sinner, John portrays God as greater than the guilt we feel for our failures. His grace is bigger than our sinfulness. For He knows all things—every sin we've ever committed and just how bad they are—and yet He loves us still. His mercy supercedes the accusings of our conscience. To believe that we are fully known by God, and yet fully loved by Him, is the essence of our healing. In this way, grace conquers our sin and guilt.

Having covered this crucial territory, we are now prepared to receive the heart-healing of our Great Psychiatrist. Please take this matter very seriously. Pause right now in the privacy of your inner person and confess the truth about yourself and the truth about God. "And ye shall know the truth, and the truth shall make you free" (John 8:32).

Confess: I am a deceived and desperate sinner. My mind is deranged with dark pictures of God. So rebellious and self-willed am I! My heart is deeply wounded with guilt and shame. The fear created by the lies I have believed make me want to hide from God and never face Him.

And yet, confess the greater reality: I now come out of hiding because I hear sweet mercy in His voice. Could it be true that He calls out to Me with a longing to embrace and heal rather than condemn and destroy? Yes, I believe it is true. I can feel His grace superabounding over my sin. My heart does condemn me, but He does not, and so I choose to rest in His love and flee from my sin and shame.

Healer of my soul: Heal every person who reads in this book of the boundless, changeless truth of Your grace. Help them, as You help me, to believe that You are truly greater in grace than all the guilt of their sins. In Christ alone I cease to hide. Amen.

13
A CAPTIVATING LIBERATION

HOPEFULLY A CERTAIN young man won't mind me telling this story. It could be kind of embarrassing, so I'll conceal his identity by calling him William, emphasis on Will, due to the fact that he was about nine-tenths will and only one-tenth whatever else makes up a human being.

One day, 15-year-old Will was taken captive by his strong will. So he decided to take my car for a spin . . . my new car, the only new car I had ever actually bought new; my car that I still owed thousands of dollars on; my car that I had carefully selected from among all the lesser competitors vying for my monthly payment; my nice car that I really, really liked more than words can tell.

Yes, that one.

And, I might add, it was the only one I had. And, I may as well add that it was a Toyota.

Yep, teenager Will decided with his wayward will to take that very car for a drive while I was two states away from my driveway—without my permission, without a driver's license and without insurance; especially without insurance. Get the picture? Sure you do. Everyone knows that a teenager driving a neighbor's car without permission, without a license, and without insurance spells trouble, everyone, that is, except the remainder of this world's teenage population.

You know what happened on the drive?

You guessed it. Will wrecked my car. (Did I mention how I felt about that car?) And he didn't *just* wreck it. He totaled it. Crushed. Smashed. Destroyed. Straight into a big ponderosa pine tree. Those trees are solid. They don't move for Toyotas. The bark was dented. That's all. Will was fine, as was the girl who took the ride with him. But my car was history. And Will was the one who did it. He knew he was the guilty party, because he was the one behind the wheel when it happened. Makes sense.

Albeit, he did it for a good cause. Something about a dog needing to be rescued from a porcupine. I've never put all the pieces together to understand how Will knew there was a dog having a porcupine problem miles away. I guess teenagers just know things like that.

Exactly!

That's just what I was thinking. Thanks for your sympathy.

I'll never forget the day a friend called with the news.

"What?" I questioned, "you mean to tell me that Will drove my car into a really big tree and totaled it?"

"Yes, that's right. I thought you should know before you get home."

My wife and I had more than a week to talk and pray about what to do. Our first impulse was, "Life is rough, kid; pay up."

There were two factors, however, that made the matter more complicated than that. First, he couldn't "pay up." He was a cashless kid. The debt was far beyond his meager financial means. No way to pay. Of course, we could impatiently wait for him to get creative. Or, we could demand that he live as our financial slave for years. But there was a second complicating factor—we loved this strong-willed, free-wheeling teenager. I mean, really loved him. And sometimes love gets painful. That is, if we keep on loving. All who love will suffer loss, and yet, their loss will be gain. We could withdraw our love and the whole matter would quickly simplify: "You blew it; you pay."

But because we knew he could not pay, and because we could not stop loving him, only one solution presented itself. To keep on loving him would require us to free Will from the debt by absorbing the loss.

After being home for a day and a half, I heard a faint, weak, guilty knock on the door. It was inevitable that Will would have to come and tell us about the accident firsthand. Now the day of uncomfortable encounter had arrived. When I opened the door, there he stood, nervous, tongue-twisted, eyes rapidly shifting anywhere but into mine.

"Hi, uh, well, um, I guess you know that I, um, well, I wrecked your car."

"Yes, that's what I've heard. I guess it's really true?"

"Yes," Will replied, closing his eyes and facing downward, "it is true."

I invited Will in. He sat across from me and Sue. Before we could speak the good news of his freedom, he began to pour forth a torrent of well thought-out promises and intentions.

"I'm gonna quit school and get a job at the lumber mill or somewhere else. Then I'm gonna sign all my paychecks over to you."

Actually, the idea was appealing. Really appealing, since we were trying to figure out the impossible math of how to keep making payments on a car that no longer had a driveable existence, and, at the same time, somehow buy another vehicle. And yet, there was the dilemma of love: absorb the loss and liberate the guilty, or cease loving and demand payment. Really, there was no way to stop loving Will. So the decision was clear. We must sustain the loss and give his world back into his hands.

"Will," I began to explain, "Sue and I have thought through this unfortunate situation very carefully, and we've come to a firm decision. We are very happy to tell you that you have no debt with us. You owe us absolutely nothing. It is not our desire that you quit school in order to get a job. We can cope with this loss. You can't. It's bigger than you are, but it's not bigger than we are. We want you to be free from this weight and continue on with life as though it never happened."

For the first time, Will looked up and got eye contact with me.

"No way!" he argued with a painful passion. "You can't do that!"

"Not only can we, but we have. You are forgiven. It's our car. We can do whatever we want with it, and we've decided to give it to you."

It was very difficult for Will to process and accept our forgiveness. But deep inside he knew the debt was bigger than he could handle, and he knew we had the power to liberate him. So, after some tears, the matter was resolved. We had made Will free in our hearts and he now accepted his freedom into his own heart.

Then we noticed something very powerful. While Will was free in one sense, we could see that he was held captive with a new kind of captivity, a liberated captivity, if you don't mind me saying it that way. Before he knew anything of our pardon, he was driven by a sense of bondage to guilt to pay the unpayable debt. After realizing that our forgiveness had released him from any obligation to pay, he was now determined out of gratitude to figure out a way to restore our loss. No longer driven by guilt, he was now motivated by appreciation.

One day Will came to me with a friend by his side, a friend who happened to be bigger than his debt. Will had entered into an agreement with this extremely largehearted person. The man explained:

"Will has told me of his accident with your car. He realizes that you have erased the debt, but he wants to make restitution. Because he has no way to do this on his own, I'm going to help him. Will is going to work for me through the summer, and I will buy you a car to replace the one you have lost."

Needless to say, I was perhaps as dumbfounded by this offer as Will was by our forgiveness. Mercy had proven itself to be powerful enough to work out justice.

A couple of years later, Will did get a driver's license. But he didn't have a car yet. One day he asked his mom if he could borrow her car to meet an appointment. While he regularly used her car, on this occasion she had to decline due to an appointment she had which overlapped with his. I happened to overhear the conversation. Partly for personal amusement and partly because he needed a car, I dangled my keys in front of his face and said,

"Hey, Will, take my car. I won't be needing it for a few hours."

The look on his face was a mixture of stomach flu and roller coaster.

"No way! I'm not interested at all in driving your car."

"Ah, come on, Will, drive it."

After a little more coaxing, Will took the keys in hand and got behind the wheel. It was interesting to see how a person drives someone else's car after totaling their previous one. I have never seen anyone back out of a parking spot with the emergency lights flashing. He drove away at about ten miles per hour, hitting the brakes every five feet or so. Will turned out to be one of the most careful drivers I know, at least in my car. (Hey, Will, how's your driving these days?)

This is exactly how grace works in God's plan for our salvation. It simultaneously liberates and captivates. We are at once free from the requirements of the law to earn salvation, and yet find ourselves eagerly delighted to obey His every word. God saves us wholly by grace, apart from obedience to His law. But in the receiving of His grace is present the desire and power to bring the life into harmony with His law of love.

"We have received grace . . . for obedience to the faith" (Romans 1:5).

"The truth of the gospel . . . bringeth forth fruit, as it doth also in you, since the day ye heard of it, and knew the grace of God in truth" (Colossians 1:5, 6).

"God is able to make all grace abound toward you; that ye, always having all sufficiency in all things, may abound to every good work" (2 Corinthians 9:8).

"For the grace of God has appeared, bringing salvation to all men, instructing us to deny ungodliness and worldly desires and to live sensibly, righteously and godly in the present age, looking for the blessed hope and the appearing of the glory of our great God and Savior, Christ Jesus; who gave Himself for us, that He might redeem us from every lawless deed and purify for Himself a people for His own possession, zealous for good deeds" (Titus 2:11-14, NASB).

In all of these scriptures there is evident a vital link between grace and godly living (obedience, good works, fruitfulness, etc.). Overcoming sin is not merely a matter of taking note of God's requirements and forbiddings and then trying our hardest to comply. Outside of a distinct consciousness of God's free grace, which has saved us while we were yet in sin, we have absolutely no hope of ever truly getting out of our entanglement with sin. The moment we step out of grace, entertaining thoughts or feelings of obligation to keep the law for salvation, true obedience to the law becomes a virtual impossibility. This is because we humans are governed by one of two motives: either love or selfishness. Obedience to the law and victory over sin are only born of the love motive. To know that God saves us without the deeds of the law communicates to the soul an accurate conception of God's love. That understanding, in turn, frees the soul from self-centered motivation. "Christ's love compels" the receivers to "no longer live for themselves, but for him who died for them and was raised again" (2 Corinthians 5:14, 15, NIV).

When we know we are not required to obey in exchange for salvation, obedience is removed from the conceptual realm of self-preservation and placed in the new context of love for the Savior. Grace cleanses the heart from the fear of being lost and from the desire to gain the rewards of heaven as the paramount motives for serving God; then, that same grace escorts the believer into the liberating selflessness of living to please and glorify God. Abiding in grace, there is no talk of what I have to do in order to make it to heaven. There is no anxiety from trying to measure up in time to squeak through the pearly gates at the Second Coming. "I had better do this or that or the other thing if I want to be saved and escape hell," gives way to an urgent, eager passion to bring honor to Christ and relieve Him of the agony that pierces His heart when we sin. Our new language is, "I *long* to live for Him. I *want* to obey His Word. I *desire* to put out of my life the sin that crucified the Lover of my soul."

We drive carefully because we have been freely forgiven for the wreck we have made of our lives.

Lord of Amazing Grace: Truly my debt is far greater than I can ever repay. And yet, I sense in my soul an anxiousness that I must somehow make up for all the horrible things I have done. Then I look at You. What I see bows me deep with humble astonishment. Just moments ago I couldn't even lift my eyes to meet Yours. But now, as I hear Your tender voice speaking my liberating pardon, through tears of joy I look up and discover a smile on Your face, as though I have never done a thing wrong. O, how I love You. I am free and yet bound, liberated and yet captivated. I am let go and yet I return. I cling to You. I pray in the beautiful light of Your love in Christ. Amen.

14
LINDA'S HARD EASY LIST

Y OU ARE NOT GONNA believe the story I'm about to tell you. But that's OK because it's not true. The point it makes, however, is very true. So true, in fact, that if you believe it, a deep peace and a high joy will grip your heart.

Linda was one of those women who had always looked forward to being happily married. From the time she was a little girl she dreamed night and day about meeting Mr. Wonderful. Oh, how she wanted to be swept off her feet by her man, whoever he might be.

And that, of course, was the curious, nagging question: Who would he be?

Who, indeed!

Well, the day of exciting encounter finally came. I wouldn't say it was love at first sight. But there was definitely something special about Herman. He was good-looking, intelligent, and charming, not to mention his cool name. But maybe he was a little too charming. The next thing Linda knew, she was head-over-heels in love. Herman proposed. She said "Yes," and the knot was tied.

On the morning after the honeymoon, another knot was tied, one in Linda's stomach that would get progressively tighter with each passing day. It all began when Hermie-cuddles (an affectionate nickname Linda would soon drop) jumped out of bed bright and early, at 5:30 A.M., and announced, "Wake up, Linda, the honeymoon is over!"

And, boy, was it. They packed the car and drove to their new home, where, upon entering, Herman handed Linda a piece of paper and said, "Read it quickly—are you a speed reader?—'cause we're running a bit behind schedule and need to get started."

And that's exactly what the paper was—a schedule. A schedule with Linda's name on it. A detailed schedule specifying her daily duties for two weeks.

"Don't worry that it's only for two weeks," Herman explained. "I'll have a new one ready for you at the end of each two-week period."

Linda was about to ask, "Are you serious?" But she got a distinct feeling inside, a sick feeling, that he was absolutely dead serious. She didn't know whether to laugh or cry or run. Her emotions fluctuated for a few moments between suicidal and homicidal.

"Well, you had better get started, Sweetheart. Time's a wastin'," Herman said as he headed out the door.

Here is an authentic reproduction of one of the lists:

Linda's List—March 1-14

5:30 A.M.—Rise and shower.

6:00—Begin breakfast (menu attached).

6:15—Awaken Hermie-cuddles with a gentle kiss and turn on shower for him.

6:45—Serve breakfast (don't forget the grapefruit juice).

7:15—Begin breakfast cleanup while husband brushes teeth.

7:25—Meet husband at front door with appropriate jacket in hand (pay attention to the weather). Say goodbye with a smile and a kiss.

7:30—Finish breakfast cleanup.

8:00—Free time.

8:15—Housecleaning (cleaning supply list and more detailed instructions attached):

> Monday—North rooms
>
> Tuesday—East rooms
>
> Wednesday—South rooms
>
> Thursday—West rooms
>
> Friday—Garage

11:00—Balance checkbook.

12 noon—Have lunch; whatever you'd like to eat, except marked items.

12:30 P.M.—Miscellaneous duties:

> Monday—Car maintenance appointments; wash car.
>
> Tuesday—Dry cleaning and banking.
>
> Wednesday— Shopping (list attached).
>
> Thursday—Wash windows.
>
> Friday—Yard work.

3:30—Dinner preparation (see attached menu).

4:30—Meet husband at door with a smile and a kiss,
   and hang his coat.
5:00—Serve dinner.
5:45—Dinner cleanup.
6:15—Free time (see list of suggestions).
6:45—Draw bath for husband.
7:00—Next day's ironing.
7:45—Hand husband towel as he exits bath.
8:00—Neck and back massage for the man of your dreams.
9:00—Lights out. "Pleasant dreams, Sweetheart!"

Dreams?

Yes.

Pleasant?

No.

Linda tried to fulfill the lists as hard as a person can try when they really don't want to. None of her efforts were ever good enough. Herman always noticed some area of failure to point out. Strangely enough, the more she determined to try harder, the less she really tried.

Ten years passed and Linda often wept in her free time. Then one day Herman dropped dead. I'm not sure of the cause. Linda was so confused in her emotions. She didn't know whether to say, "Oh, no!" and cry, or say "Yippy!" and jump for joy. Of course, once her emotions evened out, she knew the proper thing to do was mourn. So she did, as best she could.

It would be an extreme understatement to say Linda was not at all interested in ever getting married again. But time heals and soon she found herself again hopeful that she might someday meet

Mr. Right. And guess what? She did. His name was Michael. He was a great guy. The relationship moved slowly, however, which should be expected after what Linda had been through with Hardcore Herman. But with time, as they got to know each other, it became clear that Michael was a wonderful man with no hidden surprises. The day came when he proposed, Linda accepted, and they were married.

The morning after the honeymoon was a little stressful. You can't blame Linda for jumping out of bed at 5:30 A.M., half-conscious, with her clinched fists swinging in Michael's direction. Once she was fully awake, she calmed down. But when Michael handed her a piece of paper, she grabbed it, tore it in half and said, "No way, buddy!" Michael explained that it was a special love poem he had written for her. She apologized, taped the poem back together, read it with tears and realized that Michael was not Herman the Horrible.

As the years passed—with Michael sometimes waking up early to serve Linda a surprise breakfast in bed, always eager to help with the household duties, and never composing any lists for her— something strange but pleasant happened to Linda. While Michael was at work one day, she was doing some spring cleaning. On her knees in the attic, rummaging through some old boxes, she came across a shoebox full of the old lists Herman had written for her. As she read through a few of them, an old knot began to form in her stomach. Then a realization dawned on her:

"I do many of these things for Michael, and hardly even think about it."

It seemed to Linda that while she had labored to fulfill the list for Herman, she could never really do any of it quite right and was always anxious and unhappy trying. With Michael, life was totally different. It was as if he never required anything of her, but was himself continually giving; and because of his giving, she almost unconsciously, and for sure spontaneously, went out of her way to please him. Linda sighed deeply and shed a few tears of restful joy.

The same list. At one time, under Herman's ruthless rule, it appeared hard, even impossible. At another time, under the influence of Michael's love, the list looked easy, even pleasant.

Whether living for God is hard or easy is all a matter of one's perception of the Lawgiver. If you see God as One making demands upon you greater than what He Himself has given, then you will unavoidably find your efforts to keep His high and holy law a grueling, resentful task. The harder you try, the more difficult the job will become, until you finally give up in despair. The reason why is because you are laboring as a slave rather than relating as a friend (John 15:15); not because God is a slave driver, but because you think He is. You are trying to placate a God whom you don't really love at heart, even though you may say you do. But you can't love Him, because the person you imagine Him to be makes love impossible.

On the other hand, if you serve God in the light of the Cross, cultivating an ever-deepening sense of His great, self-sacrificing love for you, you will find yourself eagerly seeking to know His will and delighting to perform it.

Allow Paul to explain:

"For the woman who has a husband is bound by the law to her husband as long as he lives. But if the husband dies, she is released from the law of her husband. . . . Therefore, my brethren, you also have become dead to the law through the body of Christ, that you may be married to another—to Him who was raised from the dead, that we should bear fruit to God. For when we were in the flesh, the sinful passions which were aroused by the law were at work in our members to bear fruit to death. But now we have been delivered from the law, having died to what we were held by, so that we should serve in the newness of the Spirit and not in the oldness of the letter" (Romans 7:2, 4-6, NKJV).

According to this passage of Scripture, there are two ways a person may endeavor to serve God: "in the oldness of the letter" or "in newness of the Spirit." Paul defines the "letter" approach in contrast to the "Spirit" approach in 2 Corinthians 3:6-18. We are serving the letter when we try to obey the requirements of the law under the driving motivation of "condemnation," while remaining "blinded" to the free gift of "righteousness" given in Christ. In this frame of mind, we know what God requires and forbids, but we don't know God Himself as He is revealed in Christ. We assess the demands of the law and apply ourselves to the task of keeping it, assuming with varying degrees of legalistic consciousness, that in so doing we will be made right with God in order to secure His acceptance and salvation. I say with varying degrees of consciousness, because almost no one who is a legalist is fully aware of the fact, if aware at all. On an intellectual level the free grace of God in Christ is usually acknowledged, but on an emotional level there is anxiety and fear of losing God's favor and being lost.

Serving God in "newness of the Spirit" is an entirely different way of relating to God. The condemnation of the law is not the driving, motivational impetus, but rather the self-sacrificing love of Christ. We do not try to obey the law as a means of winning

God's acceptance, for in Christ we see that we already have it. And then, strangely enough, or not so strangely, while moving our focus from law keeping to the free grace of Christ, we find ourselves doing the very things on God's list that we could never do before. "We all, with unveiled face [no longer afraid of God], beholding as in a mirror the glory [character] of the Lord, are being transformed into the same image from glory to glory" (2 Corinthians 3:18, NKJV). Transformation is inevitable when the character of God is our focus.

By using the word *inevitable* I do not mean *automatic,* in the sense of effortless or without need of participation on the part of the one who obeys. I use the word *inevitable* to make a theological point, not a practical one. Obedience is inevitable for the true believer, in the sense that obedience certainly will be the fruitage of genuine faith that has assimilated the grace of God. Biblical faith is mutually exclusive from disobedience to God's will. "Faith without works is dead" (James 2:20). If you claim to be living by faith, and yet, willfully live in sin, your faith is a lie. Obedience to God's law is the inevitable outcome of saving faith.

To say that obedience is *automatic* is going a step too far. Automatic implies that the actual obeying occurs without any action of the will. To the contrary, it is the will that is inevitably aroused by grace. Faith itself involves the action of the will. I do not say that God's love makes obedience automatic, but that God's love inevitably motivates us to obedience.

I think Augustine was onto something when he said, "Love God and do as you please." The idea being, that truly loving God will cause me to be pleased to do as He pleases me to do. My pleasure and God's pleasure intersect in harmonious unison. There is no such thing as love for God that is knowingly disobedient to the good pleasure of His will, for "we have received grace . . . for obedience" (Romans 1:5). Obedience to God is inherent in grace. There is no such thing as cheap grace. Grace, in fact, is very costly. It cost God the life of His dearly beloved Son. And it will cost everyone who receives it everything they have and are. But here's the wonderful thing: the heart-transforming beauty of God's grace will make it our highest pleasure to give Him all we have and are, so that, when obeying Him, we shall be but carrying out our own impulses. Duty becomes a delight and sacrifice a pleasure.

Will there be hard things to do while abiding in grace? Yes, without question. But even the hard duties will be easy in view of the cross of Christ. Thus Jesus could say without contradiction, "Straight is the gate, and narrow is the way, which leadeth unto life" (Matthew 7:14). And then, paradoxically, "Come unto me, all ye that labor and are heavy laden, and I will give you rest. Take my yoke upon you, and learn of me; for I am meek and lowly in heart: and ye shall find rest unto your souls. For my yoke is easy, and my burden is light" (Matthew 11:28-30).

If you feel that your Christian experience is like having a hard To-Do list hanging over your head, then you are married to the wrong person.

If you feel that God is demanding much but giving little, then you are married to the wrong concept of God and what He wants to do in your life.

If you feel a nagging anxiety and fear about your standing with God, constantly wondering if He accepts you or not, then you are married to the idea that law keeping is the way to be saved, rather than to a God of saving grace.

Your present husband needs to die so you can be remarried to Christ, in whom the liberating grace of God is embodied. You need to "become dead to the law by the body of Christ; that ye should be married to another, even to him who is raised from the dead, that we should bring forth fruit unto God" (Romans 7:4). In other words, you need to put to death every notion that your obedience to the letter of the law will in any way, or to any degree, secure the acceptance of God. Then, you need to get remarried to the glorious truth that God has already accepted you in His beloved Son, Jesus Christ. When you shift your focus from the law to Christ, a distinct restfulness will begin to settle on your soul, and you will find yourself obeying the Lord with a whole new motive, "in newness of spirit, and not in the oldness of the letter" (Romans 7:6).

Then, one day you will be rummaging around in the attic of your memories of days gone by. You will read the old list you once labored so joylessly to fulfill. A pleasant realization will dawn upon you, and you will whisper to yourself, "I do these things for God and hardly even think about it."

God, my Husband in Christ: I have labored to no avail under anxious obligation to the law. Somehow, at least on an emotional level, I have related to You as though You were a small-minded slave driver who could be satisfied with mere compliance to the letter of the law. Now I see that Your plan for my life is so much higher and deeper than that. By giving in Christ so much more than You ask of me, You have proven Your goodness and love beyond question. As I embrace Your Son, I can sense Your grace pouring into me, freeing me from obligation to the law for salvation, and yet arousing in me more de-

sire and energy for obedience than I have ever known. My pleasure has merged with Yours in Christ. What a great way to live! I rest in Your Son. Amen.

15
THE AUTOTHEODICY OF GRACE

THEOLOGIANS GRAPPLE with what they call *theodicy*. When I first heard about this difficult issue, I thought, "Hey, I don't struggle with theodicy at all, because I don't have the foggiest idea what it is." Ignorance is bliss.

Then, I looked up the word in a few dictionaries and concluded that not only do I grapple with theodicy, but almost everyone does. It may even be *the* subject we all long to understand more than any other. See what you think. Here's the definition from two dictionaries:

"Theodicy: a vindication of God's justice in tolerating the existence of evil."

"A defense of God's goodness and omnipotence in view of the existence of evil."

It is a hard issue. Put all the factors together in one sentence and it becomes abundantly clear we are faced with an apparent contradiction: God is just and good and all-powerful while children are abused, nations are ravaged by war, and people are dying of starvation, disease, and tragedy every moment of every day.

Does the statement make sense?

Do you feel the tension?

How could God be both good and powerful and then watch a man rape a woman or a child slowly starve to death? It seems He is either good and lacking in power, or powerful but lacking in goodness.

Hence, theodicy.

Those of us who like the idea of a good and all-powerful God must try to understand and explain why such a God would tolerate even one act of injustice, let alone the myriad of such acts that have tortured our world for thousands of years. We must defend or vindicate God in the midst of the most glaring evidence in favor of His indictment. Our efforts to achieve theodicy on God's behalf take on many forms. Consider some of the most common answers to the problem. A good and all-powerful God tolerates evil:

1. to discipline us, like a parent spanks a child.

2. to punish us for our sins, like a judge imposes punishment on a criminal.

3. to teach us lessons we can only learn by pain, like a dog learns to stop barking from a shock collar.

4. to make us yearn for heaven, like a poverty-stricken African longs to live in the United States.

5. to develop character in us, like a weight trainer builds muscle by means of resistance.

There is insight to be gained from a development of these answers. But I won't deal with any of these here. Rather, I would like to suggest a rarely developed answer. And I'd like to do so by introducing a new word:

Autotheodicy.

Don't be bothered by the fact that you can't find this word in the dictionary. It's not there. I made it up. Every word has to have a beginning. This one has its birth right here. The definition is obvious. If theodicy is the human effort to vindicate God's goodness and omnipotence in tolerating evil, then autotheodicy is God vindicating Himself against the backdrop of evil. It's like the difference between a biography and an autobiography. The first is a person's life story as told by someone else. The second is a person's life story as told by himself. Perhaps God has vindicated, and is vindicating, Himself by means of a power which at first glance doesn't look all that powerful. But before we look any more specifically at God's autotheodicy—God's own vindication of His character—we must first consider the background that has created the need for His vindication.

Going all the way back to the beginning of evil in the universe, we learn that the very nature of the sin problem made it necessary for God to refrain from stopping it in its tracks by means of swift justice. The biblical account is as follows:

"There was war in heaven: Michael and his angels fought against the dragon; and the dragon fought and his angels, and prevailed not; neither was their place found any more in heaven. And the great dragon was cast out, that old serpent, called the Devil, and Satan, which deceiveth the whole world: he was cast out into the earth, and his angels were cast out with him" (Revelation 12:7-9).

What kind of images come to mind when you read the

historical record of this war? Do you picture angels clashing in space with swords or laser beams? Do you imagine the good angels finally capturing Satan and throwing him out of some region of the sky or off some far away celestial planet; and then, hurling through space, he lands in a puff of dust on earth? If so, banish from your mind all images of a physical battle with any kind of blood-shedding weaponry.

The word here translated "war" is the Greek word, *polemas*, from which we get the English words *polemics* and *politics*. *Polemic* means "an aggressive attack on or refutation of the opinions or principles of another. The art or practice of disputation or controversy." *Politics* means "competition between competing interest groups or individuals for power and leadership" (Webster's).

The warfare Satan has waged, and is waging, against God is not one of physical might, but rather of disputation, of argument, mind arrayed against mind, principle against principle. The devil's weapons have not been those of military combat, but of artifice and deceit. It is a war whose weapons are words and ideas. It is a political battle for the leadership of the universe. Satan has challenged the character of God, forging deceptive arguments against the way the Creator governs the universe.

It is logical, then, that the One fighting in God's defense is "Michael," for *Michael* means, *One who is like God.* Because it is a war which centers on misrepresenting God's character, it follows that the divine vindicator is One who is Himself an accurate representative of God. It makes perfect sense. The war is waged with lies about God, so the logical way for God to respond is to reveal the truth of who He is. Scripture bears out that this Michael is none other than the pre-incarnate Jesus Christ, the divine, self-existent Son of God (compare Revelation 12:7; Daniel 12:1).

You will notice that the deceiver forwarded his war against God, not on his own, but with alliances: "the dragon fought and *his angels.*" This tells us that Satan's misrepresentation of God was indeed cunning; his polemic angle was slick and crafty. He didn't openly proclaim himself a lying rebel. How else could he have gained the support of highly intelligent angelic beings?

Other places in Scripture give us insight into the exact content of Satan's finely spun character assassination of God. The first is in Genesis 3. Verse 1 uses the word "subtle" to describe Satan's approach to Eve. God had told Adam and Eve that sin would lead to death (3:3). In response, the adversary proceeded to construct a very dark picture of the Creator. "Ye shall not surely die: for God doth know that in the day ye eat thereof, then your eyes shall be opened, and ye shall be as gods, knowing good and evil" (3:4, 5). More straightly translated, "God has lied to you concerning this matter because He is utterly selfish, hoarding for Himself a much higher, more pleasurable state of being, which is available to you as well as to Him." Up to this point God had been perceived as a gracious Creator who loved His children with selfless care. But now, upon believing Satan's lie, Eve began to see God as a self-centered, untrustworthy liar, void of true love and concern for her happiness and well-being.

Job, chapter 1, bears out the same essential elements of the devil's defamation campaign against God. On this occasion he is exercising his artifice in the courts of heaven, before the unfallen intelligences of the universe. The gist of the account runs like this:

1. A heavenly meeting is convened with representatives from the various branches of God's vast creation, called "the sons of God" (1:6).

2. Satan attends the assembly. When asked by the Lord what right he has to be present, he lays claim to planet Earth as his territory (1:6, 7). The fall of Adam and Eve, their yielding to his arguments against God, obviously constituted a kind of legal take-over of this world, at least in Satan's mind.

3. The Lord basically rejects Satan's claim to dominion of Earth by pointing to a man named Job, who, the Lord claims, walks in His principles of righteousness due to the fact that he reverences God, or holds His character in high esteem (1:8).

4. Satan then rejects God's claim of love-prompted reverence as Job's motive for living in obedience to God's principles. To the contrary, the deceiver argues, Job rather serves God purely from selfish motives, for material wealth, not because God is actually worthy of such love and reverence (1:9, 10). Again, as in Genesis 3, the focal point of attack is the character of God.

5. Satan challenges that Job would immediately curse God to His face if the incentives and rewards were removed (1:11).

6. The Lord accepts the challenge by allowing Satan to wreak havoc in Job's life, effectively removing all self-serving reasons for Job's loyalty to God (1:12-19).

7. Job responds to the disasters in his life by continuing to love and worship the Lord and refrains from leveling charges or accusations against God (1:20-22).

With these two accounts of Satan's calumny against the Creator, let's come back to theodicy. How can God possibly be good and all-powerful, and yet tolerate the existence of evil? Well, think about it. If suffering had arisen as a mere glitch in the biological creation, certainly God could have simply obliterated the problem and all intelligent beings would have praised Him for His protection. But suffering arose out of sin. It did not come into being as a mere, non-intelligent malfunction. Rather, a rational, free moral agent rebelled against God's government, on the pretext that God is a self-serving tyrant who is holding intelligent beings with higher potential under His arbitrary control. So well constructed was his case that a large number of angels sided with Satan in his supposed liberation cause.

Now then, against this kind of backdrop, imagine the response of the onlooking universe if God would have simply destroyed Satan and his sympathizers as soon as they began to voice their accusations.

"Zap!"

A billow of smoke and they're gone. Then God says to everyone else, "Believe Me, they were all wrong about Me. I do truly love all of you and desire your highest happiness."

Just then one of the angels would have whispered to another, "Yeah, and if you don't believe Me, I'll destroy you!"

"Here we go again," would have become the eternal motto of the universe as one rebellion after another would have broken out.

Swift justice, as nice as it sounds at first, is not an effective way of eradicating sin and suffering from the universe. Whenever someone has a lot of power, he or she had better use it carefully, exercising restraint, especially in matters of self-defense. Otherwise, the use of power looks like self-serving, arbitrary control, and it probably is. If someone says, "I think you're a bad person and I don't trust you," and you respond with a bullet through their head, your action substantiates the accuser's claim. He may be dead, but a lot of other people are not, and they're all left with only one of two options: (1) Hate you in their hearts but serve you outwardly to save their lives, or (2) risk their lives by rebelling against you. Sincere, loyal, trusting love is not an option.

God has a wiser plan. And it's not just a plan; it is the real outworking of who He is at heart. Rather than executing swift justice, He has chosen to exercise a different kind of power. He has chosen grace as the means by which He will not only save us individually, but also save the universe for all eternity future. Paul explains:

"In Him we have redemption through His blood, the forgiveness of sins, according to the riches of His grace which He made to abound toward us in all wisdom and prudence, having made known to us the mystery of His will, according to His good pleasure which He purposed in Himself, that in the dispensation of the fullness of the times He might gather together in one all things [rational, free-will beings] in Christ, both which are in heaven and which are on earth—in Him" (Ephesians 1:7-10, NKJV).

You will notice in this section of Scripture that the exercise of grace toward sin is said to be wise and prudent on God's part. Behind grace Paul discerns a mysterious dimension to God's will. There is a purpose He is working out by means of rich grace rather than stern justice. What is that mysterious, wise purpose? What is the ultimate end goal of grace? "Namely, that the universe, all in heaven and on earth, might be brought into a unity in Christ" (NEB).

This Scripture clearly indicates that the universe at large—the inhabitants of both heaven and earth—has undergone a fracture in its unity due to the intruding element of sin.

How so?

By creating intelligent, free-will beings capable of love or rebellion, God willingly made Himself accountable to His creation, and has hinged the moral stability of the universe on the strength of His character to withstand scrutiny. The fracture occurred when one close to God, Lucifer by name, chose to misrepresent God's character in a subtle effort to dethrone the Lord and enthrone himself.

At this point God could take the apparently fast route of immediate extermination, with the inevitable uprising of one rebellion after another. Or He could pursue the longer, more painful path of grace, which would effectively eradicate evil forever, never to raise its ugly head again. By taking the time and enduring the sacrifice inherent in grace, the divine Genius has set out on a course to preserve our freedom of will, and yet remove the possibility of a second rebellion. This lofty aim could only be achieved by demonstrating, before the entire intelligent creation, that He is, contrary to the lie, a God of infinite, self-sacrificing love. Then all will voluntarily give their loyalty and trust in spontaneous reciprocation to His love, not for fear of His power over them.

We often ask, "If God is so powerful, why doesn't He just pull rank, give the orders, call the shots and immediately destroy anyone who questions His authority?"

Because God is more than powerful. He is good. It is His natural impulse to save His enemies, not destroy them. He is aiming, ultimately, to resolve the problem of sin and suffering by love, not by might.

The coexistence of evil and an Almighty God, far from proving Him unjust, actually reveals Him as a being of extremely high moral character and integrity. If He is truly good, and if it pains Him to behold the suffering inflicted on His creation by sin, then to allow it to exist says much about Him. It says that He will honor our freedom at any cost to Himself. It says He is confident enough in the integrity of His character to open Himself up to scrutiny.

On this note, One living and dying in radical self-abandonment enters the picture. He is the grace-wielding Defender of the divine character. He is Michael, the One who is like God, become Jesus Christ, the anointed Savior. For it is by the power of His likeness to God, and hence His ability to reveal God's true character, that He is able to save fallen humanity and preserve the unfallen universe from the accusing one who has been lying about God from the beginning of this political warfare.

Declaring the essence of His mission as Savior, Jesus said, "The hour [for My self-sacrificing death on the cross] is come, that the Son of man should be glorified [His character magnified]. Verily, verily, I say unto you [to explain the meaning of the sacrifice], except a corn of wheat fall into the ground and die, it abideth alone [selfishness leads to isolation]: but if it die, it bringeth forth much fruit [self-sacrificing love builds loyalty and trust]. He that loveth his life [more than others] shall lose it; and he that hateth his life [or loves it less than others] in this world shall keep it unto life eternal. . . . Now is my soul troubled [at the prospect of complete self-sacrifice]; and what shall I say? [Should I say] Father save me from this hour: but for this cause [the cause of saving others by the sacrifice of Myself] came I unto this hour. Father, glorify thy name [magnify Your truly beautiful character in this abandonment of self for the love of others]. Then came there a voice from heaven, saying, I have both glorified it [in Your selfless living], and will glorify it again [in Your selfless death]. . . . Now [as I give My life on the cross] is the judgment of this world: now shall the [usurping] prince of this world be cast out [from the sympathies of those he has deceived about God]. And I, if I be lifted up from the earth [on the cross to reveal who God really is], will draw all [the fallen and unfallen universe] unto me" (John 12:23-25, 27, 28, 31, 32).

When Jesus died on the cross, a great turning of the table occurred. A colossal shifting of evidence in God's favor was presented. The Father's character was glorified in stark contrast to Satan's misrepresentations. By deception he had claimed his position as "prince of this world." Now, by the revelation of the truth about God in Christ, Satan's political campaign was turned on its head. He was effectively "cast out," or as Paul says, "disarmed" by the Cross (Colossians 2:15, NIV). It is forever clear, beyond question, that God is love.

Why, then, if the war is won, does sin and suffering continue to flourish in our world? That's a great question, and the subject of the next chapter.

Father: Your wisdom in dealing with the sin problem is astounding. I can see that swift justice would have perpetuated rebellion. Grace is the answer. And really, it was the only answer You could give, because it is in Your heart to save and not to destroy. I, for one, am convinced of Your goodness and love. And I will spread the news to everyone I can. Thank You for making Yourself known. In Christ, I pray. Amen.

16
A MASTERPIECE
IN THE MAKING

"HEY, MISTER, got any change I can have to get something to eat?" came the young, female voice.

I had seen her in the distance, hunched down, arms wrapped around her knees as she leaned against the concrete wall. Winter was setting in. Snow flurries danced around her form.

"Do you take VISA," I replied with a smile.

"No, but if you don't have any change, I take bills," she smiled back, "ones, fives, tens, whatever you got. I haven't eaten since yesterday."

"I think I have a five-dollar bill," I said, opening my wallet and handing it to her. "But I'd like to know the name of the person I'm giving it to."

"My name is Erin, with an *E*, the girl version."

"Where do you live, Erin?"

"Mostly under bridges; sometimes behind garbage dumpsters."

"How long have you been on the streets?"

"For almost three years, since I was twelve."

"In Spokane the whole time?"

"No, mostly in Arizona and California."

"Well, things sure are different up here in the north. If it's not cold enough for you already, it's about to start getting real cold, freezing and below. Don't you have parents who want you home?"

"Are you kidding, man? My dad's a heroin addict and my mom just lets him use all our money for junk. I couldn't take watching him beat her up anymore. He beat me too. I could take that. But I couldn't see her bleedin' and cryin' one more day. So I took off, and I'm not going back."

Just then another young girl walked up, maybe a year or two older, with a drugstore bag in her hand.

"This is my friend, Carmen."

"Hi, Carmen, I'm Ty," I greeted her.

She looked away without speaking a word and started talking to Erin as though I wasn't there. Carmen was harder than Erin. She had probably been abused more.

"I got it," she opened the bag and handed a package to Erin, glancing back at me as if to say, "Get out of here."

"Oh, he's cool, Carmen," Erin said in my defense. "He gave me five bucks."

"What do you have there, some kind of medicine?" I asked.

"Yeah, it's motion sickness medicine. What do you care?" Not so pleasantly, but Carmen actually spoke to me.

"It's the only thing that stops the stress pains in my stomach," Erin explained. "It really helps. You should try it if anything bad ever happens to you."

If anything bad ever happens to me? If they only knew.

"Listen," I ventured to offer more meaningful help, "it's gonna be really cold tonight. You guys are hungry. My wife would love to meet you. She's a great cook, and we have a spare room with two beds. I have three children; one is a daughter about your age. Why don't you get off the streets for a few days, have some good food and a comfortable bed as guests in our home?"

Without a blink or hesitation Erin replied, "No thanks, mister, we're fine, but thanks for the money."

Carmen walked off, while voicing her justifiable fear, "Yeah, right, you don't wanna help us; you wanna use us to help yourself."

Crouching down in front of Erin at eye level, I extended the invitation again with a nearly pleading tone. Just then, one of the checkers stepped out of the nearby drugstore door. She casually passed us by, slowing down enough to blurt out, "Is that your daughter? I sure hope you can talk her into going home. She's been out here in front of our store for days bothering people."

"No, she's not my daughter," I yelled to the now quickly passing figure. Then I looked at Erin and said, "But I sure wish she was, because I would take her home and love her into the beautiful person I know she is."

"I like you, mister, and I'm tempted to go with you, but I don't know you. So thanks for the offer, but I'll be fine."

What a powerless feeling!

But what could I do? How could I expect them to trust me without knowing me? On the drive home I began to feel the feelings of God. Feelings of tender grace. Feelings of longing to save, up against, "No thanks. I'm fine." Feelings of desire to relieve pain and restore love in the face of a mistrustfulness that tied my hands. As I contemplated my dilemma with Erin and Carmen, and God's dilemma with all of us, a realization struck me: if they could have somehow known me, not as a well-dressed stranger detached from their pain, but as the child and teenager I once was, raised in a home of alcohol and drug abuse and violence against my own mother, then perhaps they would trust me and allow me to be their friend. To really help Erin and Carmen, they would need to know me as one who is like them, as one who has felt their pain. Then they could believe I did sincerely desire to help them and not myself at their expense.

This is why, even though the war was won at the Cross, sin and suffering continue to reign in our world. The self-sacrificing love demonstrated in Christ did triumph over evil in principle. But now there is a world that needs to be won over to the victorious revelation. There are many, like Erin and Carmen, who don't yet know God for who He really is. They don't know that infinite love resides on the throne of the universe. For them everything is still dark and foreboding. Jesus promised that their sin was condemned and conquered in His death, that Satan was overcome, and that they will be drawn to Him when He is lifted up before their searching eyes.

While God's vindication was wholly achieved in Christ, it is a vindication which God intends will have residual effects in His children. Once seen and believed, the triumph of Christ is to take form *in* us and find reflection *through* us. In His prayer before entering Gethsemane, Jesus said to the Father, "I have glorified thee on the earth . . . and I am glorified in them. . . . As thou hast sent me into the world, even so have I also sent them into the world . . . I in them, and thou in me, that they may be made perfect in one; and that the world may know that thou has sent me, and has loved them as thou hast loved me" (John 17:4, 10, 18, 23).

Notice the pattern. Jesus came to earth for the purpose of magnifying God's glory, His character. His life and death accomplished that lofty aim. Now Jesus anticipates that the glorious love we embrace in Him will be channeled through us to the world. As the Father was revealed in His Son, so the Son is to be revealed through His children, so the world might believe that Jesus was truly sent from the Father. In other words, God the Father wants the world to see in us the beautiful character of love demonstrated in Jesus.

The most ancient of all redemptive prophecies describes the victory of Christ over Satan:

"I will put enmity between you and the woman, and between your offspring and her Offspring; He will bruise and tread your head under foot, and you will lie in wait and bruise His heel" (Genesis 3:15, AB).

God is here addressing Satan. The "Offspring" of the woman who will crush Satan's head under foot is the Savior who will come.

Now notice a parallel New Testament prophecy addressed to the followers of Christ:

"I would have you wise as to what is good and guileless as to what is evil; then the God of peace will soon crush Satan under your feet. The grace of our Lord Jesus Christ be with you" (Romans 16:19, 20, RSV).

Bring these two prophecies into focus. The first foretells that Christ will crush Satan's head, suffering injury to Himself in the process. Jesus claimed this victory when He pointed to His crucifixion and said, "Now shall the prince of this world be cast out" (John 12:31). He likened Satan to "a strong man, fully armed," standing guard over "his own palace"; and He identified Himself as a man "stronger than he" who would "come upon him and overcome him," taking from Satan "all his armor in which he trusted" (Luke 11:21, 22, NKJV). Using similar language, Paul announced that Christ "disarmed the powers and authorities [of darkness]," making "a public spectacle of them, triumphing over them by the cross" (Colossians 2:15, NIV). As we learned in the previous chapter, Satan's armament is made up of well-crafted lies about the character of God, and Christ disarmed him by revealing the true character of God. Thus Jesus fulfilled the prophecy of Genesis 3:15, crushing Satan's head.

So why isn't the warfare over? Why does Satan continue to tempt and ravage our world? Because we, and the onlooking universe, await the fulfillment of the second prophecy, the one we noted in Romans 16:19, 20:

"The God of peace will soon crush Satan under your feet."

Under whose feet?

Under the feet of "the good and guileless" followers of Christ, the church! The vindicating revelation of God's glorious love manifested in Christ is to lighten the whole earth with the same glory through the body of Christ:

"That we should be to the praise of his glory" (Ephesians 1:12).

"To the intent that now unto the principalities and powers in heavenly places might be known by the church the manifold wisdom of God" (Ephesians 3:10).

"Being filled with the fruits of righteousness, which are by Jesus Christ, unto the glory and praise of God" (Philippians 1:11).

"I saw another angel come down from heaven, having great power; and the earth was lightened with his glory" (Revelation 18:1).

"Christ in you, the hope of glory" (Colossians 1:27).

Simply put, the world is eventually going to hear and encounter the truth about God, His goodness and love, through His people. The earth is to be enlightened with the glory of God's character by the church. Through the prophet Ezekiel, the Lord proclaims His plan:

"I will vindicate the holiness of My great name and separate it for its holy purpose from all that defiles it—My name, which has been profaned among the nations, which you have profaned among them—and the nations will know, understand, and realize that I am the Lord [the Sovereign Ruler, who calls forth loyalty and obedient service], when I shall be set apart by you and My holiness vindicated in you before their eyes and yours" (Ezekiel 36:23, AB).

The revelation and vindication of God's character in our lives is the ultimate end to which His grace is tending. According to the Greek dictionary in *Strong's Concordance,* grace is "the divine influence upon the heart and its reflection in the life." Paul points out that the free grace by which we are saved makes us into a masterpiece of divine artistry. Notice how he explains:

"For by grace are ye saved through faith; and that not of yourselves; it is the gift of God: not of works, lest any man should boast. For we are his workmanship, created in Christ Jesus unto good works, which God hath before ordained that we should walk in them" (Ephesians 2:8-10).

Grace is the active element here. By it we are saved. Then, under its influence, the believing human heart becomes God's "workmanship," translated from the Greek word *poiema,* from which we get the English word *poem.* The ancient Greeks used the word in a broad sense to mean any artistic production, in the form of poetic literature, sculpting, painting or music. The most encompassing English equivalent is the word *masterpiece*. The idea communicated by Paul is that God's grace shapes and molds us into a divine creation of masterful beauty.

We are His lyric to the world, speaking what He wants them to know about Himself.

We are His sculpture, revealing the lovely features of His beautiful character.

We are the canvas on which the colorful shades of His grace are blended to compose His image.

We are His masterpiece, as of yet a masterpiece in the making.

Erin and Carmen and countless others will trust God and go home with Him once they know Him. It is our high calling and joyous privilege to be the grace-shaped masterpiece through which they come to see and love Him.

God of infinite grace: On that day with Erin and Carmen, I felt just a little of Your pain. Oh, how urgently You long for the world to know You. May Your holy character of boundless love soon be vindicated through Your church. May the gentle greatness of Your love become so clear and personal in our hearts that the world, through us, might believe that Christ was sent by You. I'm so eager and yet so weak and carnal. Push me to the uttermost limits of my mental and emotional capacity to know You, and hold me up as You do. I pray in the light of Your character in Christ. Amen.